The Encaustic Materials Handbook

Leland Iron Works Press
Oregon City, Oregon

Revised for print on demand edition 2014
ISBN: 978-0-9893435-1-0

Contents

Forward to the Print on Demand Edition

In 2014, one year after releasing the Kindle edition of the *Encaustic Materials Handbook*, I realized that I wanted a copy of the book I could hold in my hands. For one thing, I never take my e-reader into the studio; I know what happens in there with all the melted wax, heating tools and pigments. For another, the images in the Kindle version, while quite good, are low-resolution and lack some of the detail of the originals.

And a book is different. I find something magical about the passage of books through time—pages smudged by graphite, hand-written notes in the margins, postcards and shopping lists stuck between the leaves. Evidence, in other words, of a book well-loved and often used.

The same recipes are included in this edition as in the Kindle version, but I added a couple of new photos and fixed the formatting and pagination. I also removed a couple of bad comma deployments. I have no idea where they came from.

Unfortunately, hyperlinks don't work on real books, so the Kindle version has a big electronic advantage. I love skipping around on those little blue links, and a clickable table of contents is one of the coolest things.

It all depends on what you want. For people who are at home in the electronic universe, check out the Kindle version of the *Encaustic Materials Handbook*. It's cheap, delivered instantly to your reading device, and fully wired with helpful links. For people who want a book they can dog-ear, spill coffee on, or press flowers into, here at last is a printable edition. Whichever type you may be, please enjoy.

Introduction

The Encaustic Materials Handbook is an outgrowth of my blog The Hive Encaustic (http://hive-encaustic.com/) which I started when I became intrigued with painting with molten wax. I had just finished an MFA program at Pacific University in writing, so I was all ready to launch into a new career as... a visual artist?

For me, making visual art was a crazy idea. I knew better from day one. You see, I grew up in a family of working artists and I had a pretty good idea what it meant to make a career in the field. And I didn't want anything to do with it.

From age six, I turned to writing as my art form. I was always more interested in what Billie Joe McAllister dropped off the Tallahatchee Bridge than in the drying time of paint. And yet... there was always something lurking out there, something that words didn't quite capture. I missed having a non-verbal meditative activity. I missed playing with things.

I read Joanne Mattera's *The Art of Encaustic Painting* and recommend it as a starting point for all encaustic artists. It gives you a good working overview of the materials and techniques, but also provides something even more valuable: other encaustic artists. In this book I saw the myriad ways that wax was used as an art material, by the famous and the unknown. By sculptors, painters and craftspeople of all kinds.

So there I was, a writer setting up an art studio and playing with melted wax. I already had a full time job, a family, and a second career as a writer. What was I doing?

Thus the blog was born—a place to ask those nagging questions, post my triumphs, confess my mistakes and try to use my writing for something while I blew off all my free time making visual art. I started with a simple question: Could a writer learn to make art using one of the trickiest (and most beautiful) mediums ever devised by those tricksy ancient Greeks? While not going broke?

If you are reading this book, you already know that making art isn't cheap. Have you ever walked out of an art supply store without dropping fifty bucks? Can't be done. The pretty colors, the goo, the nice clean brushes and the freshly-gessoed canvases whisper the siren song of money disappearing down the drain. Everyone's got a *Mona Lisa* inside them, right? Or if not a Mona, at least an Elvis on black velvet.

When a friend offered me a one-person exhibition in her shop, I thought *why not?* I started small, with melted candles and chalkboard paint on home-made boards, working over the wax layers with graphite and oil crayons. The show opened, my friends bought pieces, and I thought *wow, this art biz isn't so bad.*

But remember, I was still buying two-pound bricks of paraffin from a craft store for $15. When I went online to find cheaper materials, I found an industry of encaustic art supplies that compared favorably with raising race horses—in other words, it wasn't cheap.

At these prices, how could a beginning artist afford to make mistakes?

Fortunately for cheapskates everywhere, artists have been making their own art supplies since the first cave woman sketched a horse on a cave wall with the pointed end of a burned stick. And information about how to make your own encaustic supplies is out there too. You just have to find it.

From sources such as *A Manual of Fresco and Encaustic Painting* by William Benjamin Sarsfield Taylor, published in 1843, *Encaustic Materials and Methods* by Francis Pratt and Becca Fizell published in 1949, and *The Artist's Handbook of Materials and Techniques* by Ralph Mayer, first published in 1957, I learned there was no one way to make encaustic art, and no one source for encaustic materials. I set out, with small steps, to make my own encaustic medium, paint, supports, and grounds.

This book is the result of three years' research and experimentation with do-it-yourself encaustic materials. Encaustic art is not cheap but I can confidently say that by cutting a few corners you will save hundreds of dollars per year.

If you aren't a cheapskate like me, you can build your entire art studio from R & F Handmade Paint, as you can from most retail art supply stores. Even my old friends Swan's Candles have a full page on their web site devoted to encaustic tools and supplies.

There are plenty of times when a couple of clicks on a web site will solve all your problems. Here are just a few of those times:

When **not** to DIY:

- If you don't know whether this art form is for you;
- If you are taking a workshop and the instructor tells you to bring prepared supports to the first class;
- If encaustic is only part of a larger project;
- If you have more money than time.

On the other hand, you are a DIY encaustic materials person if:

- You love the art form but hate the cost;
- You work with large quantities of materials and don't have time for cute little tins;
- You're just a DIY person at heart;
- You've tried the rest and like your own recipe best.

Why an Encaustic Materials Handbook?

I was clicking through my blog one day looking for my weights and measures table (it's so me to arrange my world according to cat food tins, as if a can of Super Supper is the Greenwich Mean Time of measuring units) when I realized that the blog was my main reference tool. I began to think about the years I'd put into learning about grounds and gessoes, hot wax and cold wax, not to mention tools and recipes. While there are many handbooks of artist materials out there, and many encaustic technique books by talented artists, there aren't any resource texts devoted to encaustic materials and tools.

I had to write my own.

So what you hold in your hands is a cleaned up, trimmed down, enhanced, buffed and (yes) waxed version of the blog. Check the blog (http://hive-encaustic.com/) for new messy experiments, and comment freely when I get it wrong. Keep this e-book handy for recipes, tutorials, photos, and the ever useful **weights and measures table** in Appendix B at the end of this book.

Special thanks to The Theory who took all the photos and edited the text. The book would have been released weeks earlier if it hadn't been for his insistence that the images had to look good and the words had to make sense. What's up with that, anyway? Thanks, sweetie!

Encaustic Basics

The word "encaustic" comes from the Greek term *enkaustikos*, which means to burn in. It sounds so clinical. But think of a room scented with honey and warmed from tins of melting beeswax. Think of color that sits so deep in the paint that it seems to emanate from the molecules themselves. People say that encaustic art glows from within. You hear the word luminous applied to encaustic paintings.

Fayum Mummy Portraits

The first time I saw encaustic art was in a traveling exhibition of Egyptian art at the Portland Art Museum. We don't have a permanent collection of Egyptian art in Portland, and my kids and I were anxious to see anything Egyptian.

But this exhibit wasn't dynastic art—King Tut or Nefertiti or Akhenaten, or the work of the pyramid builders. Instead it was art from a much later period, when Egypt was occupied by the Roman Empire, during the time of Caesar and Cleopatra. This was a series of Fayum mummy portraits painted between AD 40 and AD 250, nearly two thousand years ago. (Roberts, p. 7)

The portraits were painted on wooden boards or linen panels, and some were still attached to mummy cases that held human remains. Each portrait was intimate and lovely, as if the dead person was staring at us through a window from the past. From the hairstyles and clothing, it was clear the portraits were less stylized than art from the time of the pharaohs. Each person seemed almost on the point of taking a breath.

And the paintings looked so fresh and new. As I drew closer to learn what caused this strange human connection, I saw there weren't many discernible brushstrokes in the paint. Yet the paint was deeply layered. In fact, the paint had so much depth the portraits were almost holographic. And the paint was wax—a blend of beeswax and resin called *encaustic*.

Somehow the wax had created a place *inside* the painting where the person still lived. I didn't know what encaustic was, but I was hooked.

Greek Encaustic Art

Although the ancient Egyptians were master beekeepers, we think the ancient Greeks were among the first to use wax in their paintings. Although very little remains, we know from historical accounts that the Greeks used both encaustic and fresco for their large wall murals, but may have preferred encaustic because it offered the richest and most light-fast colors and actually helped to stabilized the walls upon which the murals were painted. (Taylor, pp. 126-127)

Despite the fact that wax can crack and melt, it can be as strong as the ages when properly prepared and applied. Beeswax was used to seal the hulls of ancient ships—and how do we know? Because in ships excavated from the sea, the wax is still intact.

What did the term *enkaustikos* or "to burn in" actually mean to the ancient Greeks?

Of course the Greeks didn't have electric palettes or hot plates, so they had to melt their wax over fire. Some of the few surviving records of artists using the encaustic process come to us from Hellenic vase art. There we see artists holding tiny pots of encaustic paint in one hand and applying dabs of hot wax with the other while their assistants tended the charcoal braziers that kept the wax warm.

Then as today, applying melted wax requires both speed and precision. Speed because (as any child learns when playing with candles at the dinner table) wax cools almost immediately. Precision because once cooled, wax stays where you put it. The artist has to be right the first time.

But the painting isn't stable until a blast of heat fuses the surface layer of wax to layer beneath it. And although this is *hot* heat, it can't be so intense that it liquefies the wax and ruins the painting. It is heat precisely applied at just the right temperature, for just the right amount of time.

Burning in or fusing the final coat of wax on a large wall mural must have required nerves of steel. They suspended charcoal braziers from scaffolding in front of the mural, fusing a section of the painting at a time. One ancient Greek artist called Lysippus actually added an inscription beneath a mural stating that he himself had burned-in the painting. (Taylor, p. 6)

Encaustic art was almost lost after the fall of the Roman Empire, and practiced in only isolated areas. It wasn't until the discovery of Pompeii and Herculaneum, two Roman cities that were consumed in a volcanic eruption, that encaustic painting came to the attention of European painters. (Stavitsky, p. 7) Fragments of encaustic murals actually survived the heated ash and pumice that buried the cities, and their brilliant colors encouraged new experimentation with the medium.

Contemporary Encaustic Art

Jasper Johns and Brice Marden are two contemporary artists associated with encaustic materials. But even before Johns took up the heated palette, many American and European artists had begun experimenting with wax painting. The advent of electricity and our handy electric gadgets provided the greatest change in the medium in thousands of years.

Ralph Mayer in *The Artist's Handbook of Materials and Techniques* summarizes the change like this:

"The greatest deterrents to its [encaustic] use in the past has been the cumbersome charcoal-fired heating arrangements which were not very much improved two hundred years ago over what they were two thousand years ago. Today the use of electrically heated equipment has changed the process to one that is relatively convenient." (Mayer, p. 356)

Beeswax, Paraffin and Plant Wax

I got started in the wax trade as a kid, playing with my parents' dinner candles during really boring conversations. Candles are addictive—fire, molten wax, and the thrill of getting away with something while your parents aren't watching. I waited until the plain white paraffin tapers had burned down until chandeliers of drip art were hanging off the candles' sides. I would reach up, snap off a section, and plunge it back into the flame. I usually got this far before my mother caught me.

In its most basic form, encaustic paint is melted beeswax mixed with pigment. Dry pigment powder or oil paint are the usual color additives. The artist melts the wax on a hot plate or palette, adds pigment, and applies the paint by brush to a prepared surface.

Over the centuries, different methods have been used to extend the melting temperature of wax. Although beeswax melts between 140 and 147 degrees F, wax begins to soften at even lower temperatures. A warm room, for instance, or placement next to sunny window can damage encaustic art. Whole encaustic paintings have been known to slide off their supports if the wax melted and the support underneath didn't offer enough adhesion.

To solve this problem, artists have blended beeswax with harder substances like pitch and resin which extend the melting point of the wax and help to keep the painting stable. Damar resin is the most common additive, which adds a glossy finish and retards the foggy white surface crystallization called "bloom."

The method I will discuss most fully in this book is the most common—classic—hot wax-damar resin blend. You can buy it pre-made and ready to melt from a variety of brick-and-mortar or online resources. Or you can make your own, experimenting with different amounts of damar to find the consistency you like best, at a substantially reduced price.

But I am including cold wax too, which may not be strictly encaustic, at least the way the ancient Greeks meant it, but is a versatile addition to encaustic materials.

Beeswax

You got it—beeswax is made by bees. Wax is the basic structure of a bee's hive, the comb. The busy little guys build perfect six-sides cells in which to store their honey or incubate their eggs. Wax can be golden in color or dark and pitchy, depending on whether it contained honey or larvae. When beekeepers harvest honey and wax from a hive, the product is stained with all kinds of detritus from the lives of bees. A first rough filtering catches those large impurities.

Yellow beeswax

I love filtered yellow beeswax, and not just because it smells good! By itself, without any added damar resin, yellow beeswax is a perfect base layer for encaustic paintings. When used to make encaustic paint, especially yellow and red colors, it imparts a deep golden glow. I like to have a pound of rough filtered yellow wax in the drawer as well as a couple of pounds made into encaustic medium.

Where to buy yellow beeswax

Visit your local beekeeping supply for rough-filtered yellow wax. You can buy it online, but a visit to a beekeeping supply is worth the trip for so many reasons—not the least of which is the opportunity to buy local honey. I go to Ruhl Bee Supply in Gladstone, Oregon. They sell everything a modern beekeeper needs, and there's no better place to go to connect with the small creatures who pollinate our crops and create honey and wax. See **Appendix D: Encaustic Supplies** for more information about where to buy wax.

Ruhl Bee Supply's one pound block of yellow beeswax sells for $7.25. It is a light medium yellow and smells of honey *a lot*. Cooked with damar resin, this wax makes an excellent base coat or primer because it remains flexible and sticky.

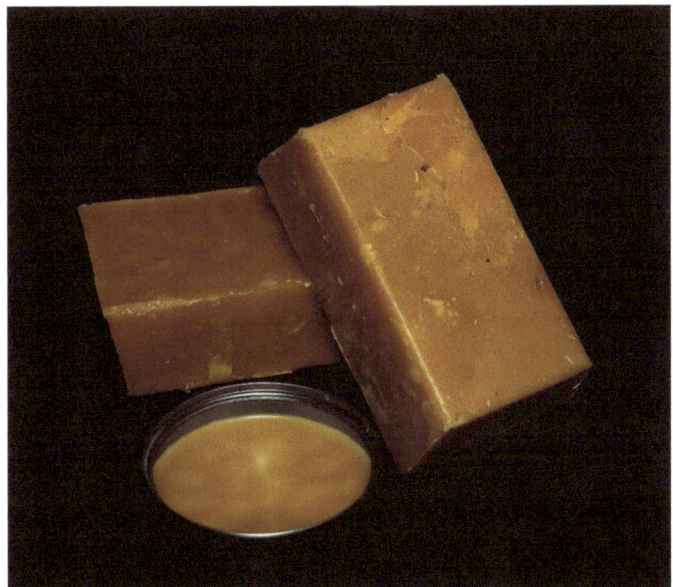

Luscious, swoon-worthy unrefined yellow beeswax in one-pound bricks. The tin contains yellow wax medium.

You can buy refined yellow wax, which comes in an easy-to-use granulated form. It clouds less than the rough filtered stuff I use and blends well with pigments. Yellow wax is beautiful, but sometimes it feels like there's a fog surrounding each color molecule. You will experiment and find those times when you want this effect.

You can get more highly filtered and refined yellow wax from art supply stores or candle-making resources. Since I prefer the raw stuff, I usually skip the refined yellow and go straight to….

White beeswax, refined

This is the stuff of which dreams are made, creamy white, smooth, and translucent. Believe it or not, beeswax comes out of the bee nearly white, and it is only the presence of pollen, honey, baby bees and bee dirt that turns it yellow. So you want to find a supplier that does not bleach its wax, but filters and filters and filters again to get that silky pure white product.

Cosmetic grade wax comes to you as pellets or in granulated form called *prill*. When you buy wax for the first time, please note that the first listings on any web site or art supply store will be for *wax medium*. Check the ingredients list. If the product contains any kind of resin or carnauba wax, you are looking at a pre-mixed substance that can be melted on your palette and used immediately. No additional preparation is needed. Wax medium generally costs twice what the raw ingredients cost. If you are new to encaustic and just want to feel it out, I suggest you buy the medium and get to work. But if you are a cheapskate like myself, want to understand the materials, or wish to adapt standard recipes to your own purposes, scroll down the web listing until you find less expensive pure beeswax products.

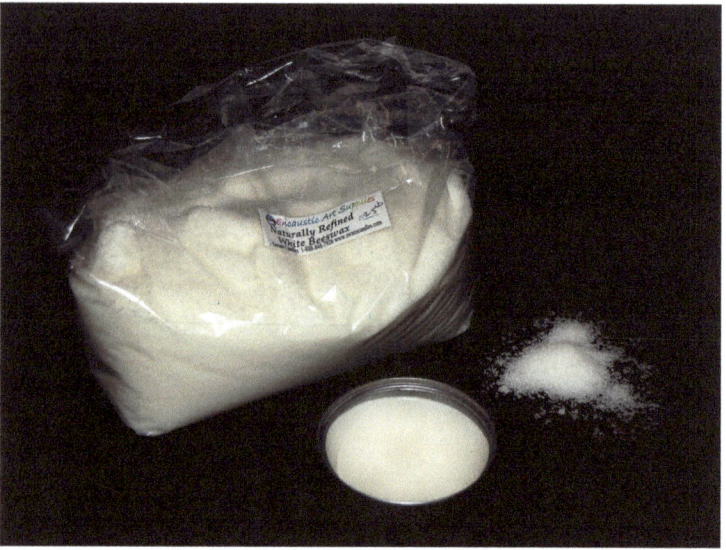

THE stuff... a five pound bag of refined beeswax, tin of white wax medium and a handful of prill. See how tiny the specks of wax are?

Where to buy white beeswax

Beeswax is available in art supply stores in eight ounce and one pound bags, for $15 to $16 per pound. But candle-making supply stores are generally a better place to buy wax. I buy my white wax from an online company called Swan's Candles for about $8 per pound. You can get it in any quantity from 1 ounce to a 55-pound case, and they have variable shipping rates and speeds. **Appendix D: Encaustic Supplies** for more information about where to buy wax.

I found Swan's online after searching for local unbleached beeswax at a reasonable price. Because I live in rural Oregon, I could have cheap, I could have local, or I could have unbleached. But I could not have all three. That's the economy of living twenty-five miles from the nearest art supply store. Thank goodness for the internet. Swan's is located in

Lakewood, Washington; their products are completely clean and green; and the price, even with shipping, is better than okay.

Swan's offers other types of encaustic and candlemaking wax:

- Multiwax Microcrystalline wax
- Brazilian Carnauba wax flakes
- Candelilla wax flakes
- Impasto wax—modeling wax
- Paraffin waxes with various melting points
- Other natural waxes including soy and coconut
- Encaustic damar medium from 3 ounces to 10 pounds
- Encaustic carnauba medium from 3 ounces to 1 pound

Nepalese bronze-casting wax

The Newari people in the Kathmandu Valley of Nepal have a lively bronze-casting tradition. Their sculptures of Buddhist and Hindu deities are considered masterpieces, and are represented in many museums around the world. Their casting wax is a dark mixture of raw beeswax and pine pitch. It is hard, sticky and pungent. In their tradition, they use only wax extracted from *Apis dorsata*, the giant open-comb honey bee found in Nepal's Terai region. To cast sculpture, they use a lost-wax process where a wax mold is encased in dung-rich clay. The wax is melted out and molten bronze is poured into the clay mold, leaving only bronze in the mold.

Paraffin

Paraffin is the wax most often used in candles. The normal melting point is 120 degrees F, though you can get types with a melting point as high as 150 degrees F. In its solid state, paraffin is brittle and friable, prone to chipping, cracking and splitting. Paraffin isn't sticky but it possesses a certain oily touch that always feels like a candle. Yet paraffin is the clearest, most nearly transparent of all the waxes.

Paraffin is too soft to use by itself in encaustic art. Long before it gets to a sunny Palm Springs ambient temperature of 120 F, your encaustic painting will have started to soften and sag.

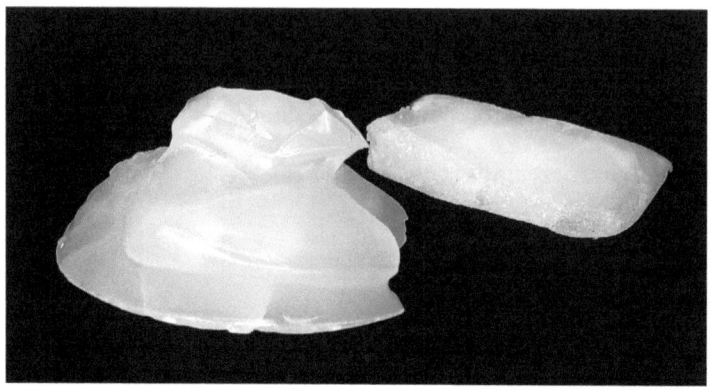

Chunks of paraffin. A good additive and extender for other types of wax. It has a lovely clarity.

We all know something else about paraffin wax, thanks to Crayola Crayons. It takes color very well. In fact you may have already learned some important lessons about pigment as a result of those third-grade art projects: some crayon colors are buttery soft and blend well while others stay hard and clumpy. This is because of how much pigment you need to add to the wax in order to create a true color.

Creating pigment has been a human pursuit for 100,000 years. Earliest forms of drawing and painting materials were as simple as the charcoal or deposits of colored clay called ochre. Now we derive pigments from plants as well as minerals, and some of the newest and brightest colors are chemical creations.

In order to fashion a deep and true color—the color you see in your mind's eye—you may need to add a lot of oil paint or dry pigment to your wax. The more secondary compounds you add to the wax, the softer and less stable your wax becomes. In a crayon, you end up with a color that glides easily and blends well. In encaustic, you may end up with a surface that remains soft or seems to take forever to cure.

Other chemically-derived waxes

Microcrystalline wax is a petroleum distillate, ranging in color from brown to white. It is often used in sculptural modeling and jewelry-making, as well as the waxed surface of hockey pucks. Montan, extracted from coal, is an extremely hard, dark wax.

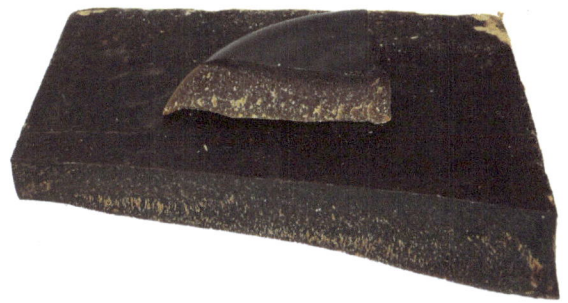

Montan wax. This industrial wax is used for casting. Artists occasionally combine it with beeswax for more flexibility.

Plant waxes

Plants of all kinds make their own waxy substance. For instance, **Carnauba wax** is made from the leaves of a palm tree found in Brazil. A natural, non-toxic wax, it is used in everything from waxy candy coating to furniture and car finishes. It is too brittle to use by itself, but it can be blended with beeswax to create a harder, glossier medium. When I first started working in encaustic, carnauba was considered non-traditional and people weren't using it much. Carnauba wax is now a standard encaustic material and pre-mixed beeswax-carnauba medium is easily available.

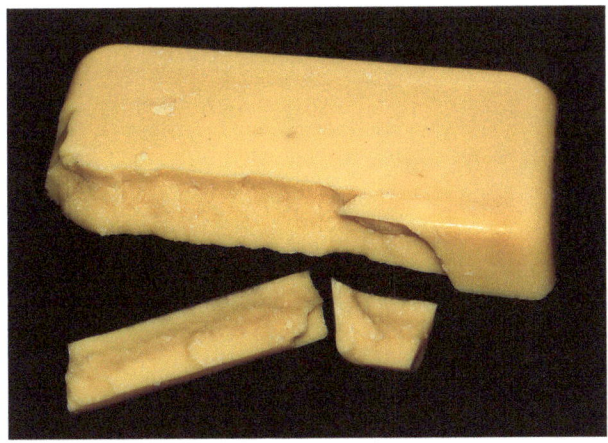

One pound of carnauba wax medium.

Other types of plant waxes include **bayberry**, **candellia**, **soy** and **coconut wax**. Candellia is another hard wax with a high melting point which can be added to beeswax, but the others have much lower temperature ranges and are better suited to other purposes. When you start making encaustic art, you will find yourself making the occasional candle—why not? As I discovered as a young thing, you can learn a lot about wax during long conversations by candlelight.

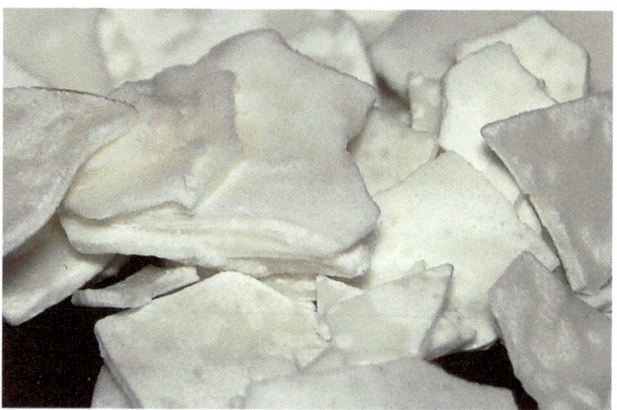

Soy wax flakes.

Wax Melting Point Chart

All temperatures in degrees Fahrenheit:

Coconut	110°F
Soy, bayberry	113°F
Paraffin, depending on wax type	120, 130, 140, 150°F
Beeswax	144-147°F
Candelilla	155-162°F
Impasto modeling wax	170°F
Microcrystalline, multiwax	175-200°F
Carnauba	179-186°F
Montan	179-200°F

Wax Medium

I confess. In my zeal to be cheap, I will launch myself into an arcane process that takes time, mental energy, and way more money than I intended to spend. I'm one of those people who will jump down the rabbit hole to Wonderland whenever the fancy strikes. That's me, professional procrastinator.

But if you are an outcome-oriented person, you may see spending an afternoon cooking wax as time away from the studio when you could be making art. For you, there are art supply stores and the internet. Review **Appendix D: Encaustic Supplies** for more information.

But if you are invested with the do-it-yourself spirit, making your own wax medium is cheap and liberating for an artist.

What is Wax Medium?

Wax medium is the main ingredient in encaustic paint. You will use far more encaustic medium than you expect—which is why most artists get in the habit of making their own.

In the next chapter we will talk about prepared surfaces for painting, but for now you need to think of your medium as that material which:

- Bonds with the underlying, non-wax **base layer** of your board, panel or support, sometimes called **GROUND**;
- Bonds with the layers of wax you will paint on top.

	Painting	
Base layer, ground or gesso		
Board, support or panel		

Cross-section of an encaustic painting.

Damar Resin

As I mentioned earlier, wax can be used by itself but most encaustic media also include a substance to extend the melting point. Many artists use damar resin, which is sap harvested from lowland rain forest trees in Malaysia. The harvesting process is like tapping for maple sugar and is, I understand, more or less sustainable. (Before we go down that road, remember that painters also use glue made from rabbit skins. It's not always pretty, this art thing.)

Damar comes in crystallized lumps and smells like tree pitch. When added to beeswax it will:

- Raise the melting point of wax;
- Create a harder, glossier surface without changing the wax's color;
- Inhibit some of the "bloom" or haze that beeswax develops over time.

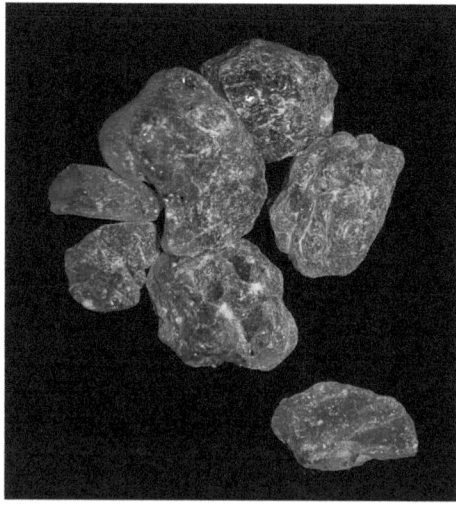

Damar crystals may LOOK like crystallized ginger but they smell like pine resin.

Where to buy damar crystals

Damar is sold in one-pound bags. Any art supply store will carry it for $10 to $16 per pound. I've had mixed luck with the cheaper resin as it sometimes comes so embedded with splinters it looks like a toothpick factory exploded in my encaustic medium. But that's why we need cheesecloth to strain it after cooking.

Note: Don't use **damar VARNISH** to make hot wax medium. The varnish form is made from turpentine and is flammable. Damar varnish is used in cold wax mediums and in mixing pigment.

Wax Medium Recipes

Basic Encaustic Medium

The most common medium is a combination of eight parts beeswax and two parts damar resin crystals. A higher percentage of damar resin (such as three parts resin to seven parts wax) will make your medium sticky and harder to work with a lower percentage won't do much to inhibit bloom. As you use each batch of wax medium, note what you like about its workability.

You will need:

- 1 pound of beeswax
- 3-4 ounces of damar crystals
- A heavy Teflon saucepan. This will be your wax pan from now on.
- Clean, dry tins. I use cat food tins, but people use muffin tins, loaf pans and those pretty little tins designed for encaustic medium. Cat food tins hold about ½ cup of wax, so plan to use five or six tins per pound of wax, depending on how full you fill them. Obviously, your mileage may vary, depending on your containers.
- Candy thermometer
- Wide-mouth funnel
- Colander or strainer with handle
- Cheesecloth, two folded 18" sections
- Wooden spoon

Before starting, cover your counter or table top with wax paper. Arrange your clean dry tins, muffin tins or loaf pans in rows, an inch or two apart. Place your wide-mouth funnel in the first tin in the first row and determine how full you want fill each tin. You can experiment by filling a tin with water to the desired level, placing the funnel in the tin and marking the water level on the inside of the funnel with a Sharpie pen. You don't want any surprises when pouring for the first time.

Choose your pour area carefully—you want to be able to move down the rows with a pan of 200 degrees F wax and not trip over anything! If you have little children underfoot or husbands or even a chatty best friend, get a sitter or wait until everyone is taking a nap. You will be working with volatile substances at significant heat. You don't want to be distracted.

Prepare your strainer by pressing your pre-cut cheesecloth into the strainer. I like to place the cheesecloth sections crosswise to one another for maximum coverage.

Step One: Place your wax, either bricks or prill, in your sauce pan over medium high heat. I have a two-quart sauce pan which cooks a pound of wax comfortably. Some people use Crock-Pots or other large capacity pots but I find Crock-Pots too heavy to lift and awkward to pour from. Make sure you are working with a pot or pan that you will be able to lift comfortably when filled with hot wax.

As soon as the wax begins to melt lower the heat to medium. You will play the heat between medium high and medium until the wax is fully melted. Use your candy thermometer to watch the temperature. Allowing your wax to overheat may discolor the medium.

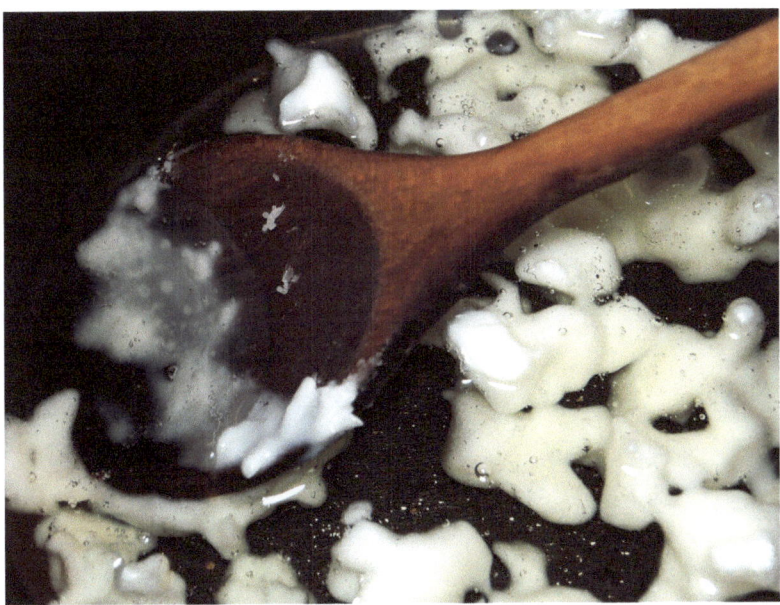

Melting white wax. This part of the process takes about ten minutes

Step Two: As soon as the wax is melted and steamy, with temperatures above 155 degrees F (and climbing) add your damar crystals to the hot wax a lump or two at a time, being careful not to splash. The crystals will spit and crackle and melt in thick ribbons. Using your wooden spoon, stir the contents in a slow circle, allowing the damar ribbons to melt into the wax. Don't be surprised if you suddenly see bits of wood in your medium. Damar resin is tapped from trees, and small twigs may get trapped in the sticky sap. The cheese cloth will strain them out.

Filtered white wax has so little scent that adding damar will fill the room with its clean pitchy aroma. Yellow, unfiltered beeswax has such a strong honeyed scent that you might not even notice the smell of pitch.

By the time the temperature reaches 180 to 190 degrees F, most of the resin will be melted and incorporated into the wax. Turn the heat down and get ready to pour.

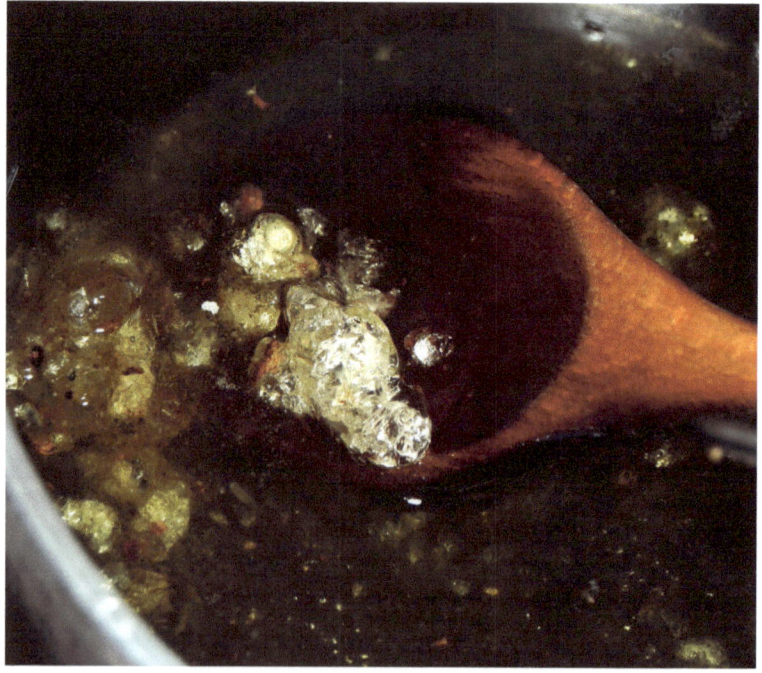

Adding lumps of damar crystal. You can already see little bits of wood floating in the wax that were embedded in the damar.

Step Three: Balance your strainer over the funnel. If you can do it, stabilize the strainer with one hand and pour with the other. If this feels awkward, ask a friend to hold the strainer. You don't want to feel awkward and you certainly don't want any surprises. Move smoothly from tin to tin. If you need a break, return the pan to your burner for a moment.

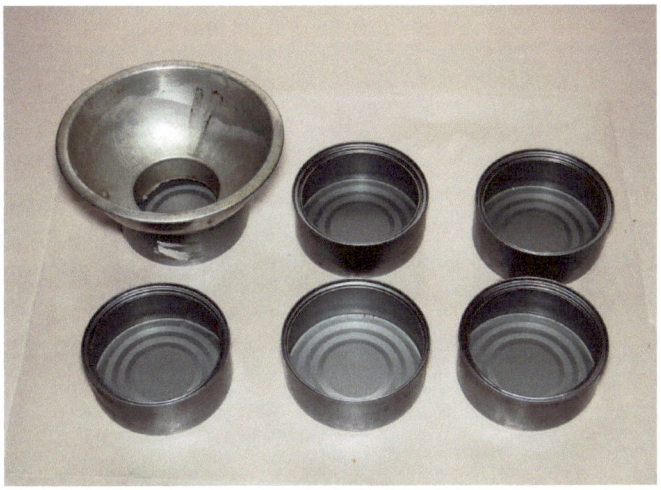

A fleet of cans and a funnel ready for medium.

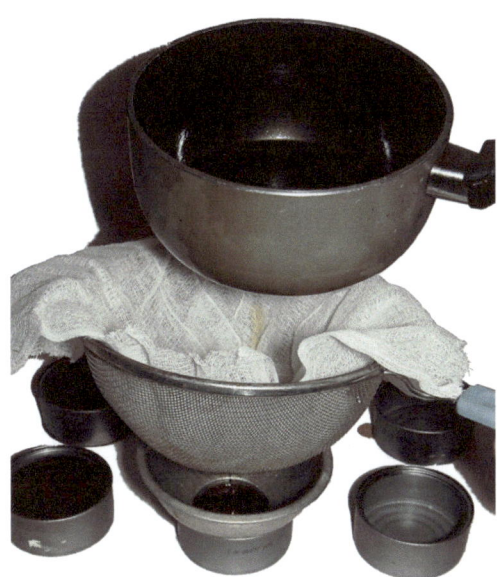

Cautiously pouring hot medium through the strainer and into the cans.

As you pour, you will see a residue of twigs and splinters collecting in your cheesecloth. When you are finished, and the cheesecloth is cool to the touch, simply drop the cheesecloth in the garbage. Unlike turpentine, mineral spirits or other art-related substances, damar and wax don't harm the environment.

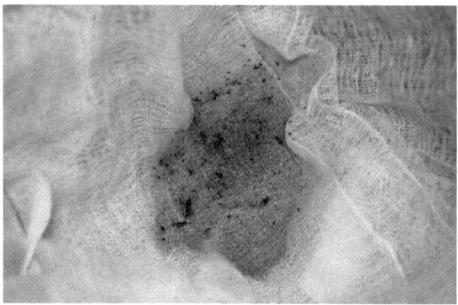

A nest of wood splinters and other gunk caught in the cheesecloth filter--and not in the medium.

Wax medium will shrink and crack as it cools. Within a couple of hours you can stack and store your medium for future use. If you poured into muffin tins, turn the pan over and strike it once or twice on the edge of a table. The wax will pop out in neat muffin shapes, ready for use. Filled tins can go directly onto your palette to be re-melted as medium and mixed for paint.

Half and Half Encaustic Medium

One cold winter in Oregon, I got tired of the bloom popping up on my encaustic pieces. It was unstoppable. I decided to experiment with different proportions of wax and resin. I came up with a seven parts wax to three parts resin recipe that balances flexibility, ease of use and bloom prevention.

But I learned that other artists had taken the proportions further in their work, one even developing an encaustic paint based on a medium that was equal parts wax and resin. You can read about **Esther Geller's paint** in the chapter on **Colors, Paints and Glazes**. Here is the medium recipe:

You will need:

- White beeswax
- Damar resin crystals
- Clean dry tins
- Your regular wax medium setup of strainer lined with cheesecloth, funnel, heavy melting pan and thermometer.

Step one: Melt 5 parts white beeswax over medium high heat until fully melted.

Step two: Add five parts damar resin crystal to melted wax, dropping the pieces into the hot mixture carefully to avoid splatter.

Step three: Continue to stir the mixture as the resin melts into thick ribbons. Watch your temperature to keep from going over 200 degrees F. The resin should be fully incorporated around 185 degrees F.

Step four: Line a strainer with cheesecloth and carefully pour the hot wax mixture through the strainer into ½ cup muffin tins. When fully cooled, turn the muffin pan upside down and strike the edge of the pan against a hard surface until the wax cakes pop out. Unlike regular wax medium, this resin-enriched recipe doesn't shrink as it cools. If they still don't pop out, try holding the pan in both hands and gently flexing the metal. Strike again.

Carnauba Wax Medium

Using carnauba wax in encaustic medium is becoming more popular. While this plant wax is brittle, it has a higher melting point than beeswax and polishes to a high gloss. I recommend experimenting with it to see if you like the effects in both the medium and the paint. You can buy beeswax-carnauba wax medium pre-mixed from most encaustic supply outlets, but here's a basic recipe just to familiarize you with the proportions:

- 9 parts beeswax
- 1 part carnauba wax

Melt the waxes together and pour into dry tins. Since the melting point of carnauba wax is 179-186 degrees F, expect the cooking process to be much like melting damar crystal. Be careful not to overheat.

Other Wax Combinations

Beeswax blends well with almost any other wax. Extending beeswax with paraffin or even microcrystalline waxes can save money. (Mattera, pp. 91-93) Experiment to see what works best for you.

Cold Wax for Encaustic

About Cold Wax

If you've read much about encaustic, you've probably heard of a cold liquefied wax called Punic Wax (Mayer, p. 442) and, like me, you dismissed it as an arcane witches brew. Pliny the Elder, who perished during the eruption of Mt. Vesuvius, left us the most detailed account of how to make Punic Wax. Essentially, it is beeswax boiled with sea water and potassium carbonate and left to bleach in the sun. The wax becomes a white paste that can be blended with oils and pigment to make paint. The term for what happens to the wax in this process is *saponification*. It becomes a compound we know as soap.

I doubted I would ever try to make cold wax paste. Why bother when hot wax gave me everything I needed—warmth, wonderful aromas, and daily challenges?

But while I was researching Greek mural art, I came across cold wax paste again. As I described earlier, the Greeks loved encaustic for their wall murals. Wax was not only permanent and light-fast, but also strengthened the surface to which it was applied. Because walls are large surfaces to cover with hot wax, they used a method of heating the wall in sections and applying initial coats of wax to prime the surface. (Taylor, pp. 137-140) The wax concoction they used was a cold wax paste—mostly to address the fact that stone heats and cools very slowly—but also to achieve the kind of surface saturation that they needed to create a permanent ground for their painting.

The Ancient Greeks and mural art

For their murals, the Greeks didn't just heat their wax—they heated their walls. (Taylor, p. 135) They started with a clean but not polished stone wall. They built large moveable scaffolding from which they could suspend a charcoal-fired brazier which hung close to, but not touching, the surface of the wall. The artist heated the wall in sections until it reached about 100 degrees F. Once a section was properly heated, the artist applied a cold wax emulsion to the stone. The process was repeated over and over again, maintaining the heat level, until the stone wall couldn't absorb any more.

Using cold wax in this context makes a lot of sense. When working on a surface as big as a wall, on a material as chilly as stone, the application of melted wax would be somewhat tricky. Heating the wall to temperatures sufficient to absorb melted beeswax, somewhere around 145 to 150 degrees Fahrenheit, could crack or damage the stone or burn your villa to the ground. As we know, beeswax also cools quickly, especially when applied to a cold surface. Hot beeswax wouldn't penetrate cold, or even slightly warmed, stone very effectively, and would in fact be about as permanent as candle wax drippings. Artists needed a substance that would penetrate the stone and provide a ground for the wax painting to cling to.

Cold wax paste, which is already in a more or less liquid state, glides onto warm stone easily. In fact, the wall doesn't need to be much more than simply hot to the touch for the paste to penetrate. As wax soaks into the wall, it drives out air and gas that might bubble up later during the painting process—causing those irritating pinholes.

After the wall cooled, which could take several days, it would still look wet and a waxy residue would remain on the surface. This was the perfect ground to receive hot wax encaustic paint. The hot wax bonded with the wax-saturated stone, creating a permanent surface. Once the painting was finished, the artist covered the whole surface with another layer of clear wax and burned in—fused—the final layer, using the same suspended brazier method as before.

Cold Wax in Contemporary Encaustic Practice

I don't know of many artists doing large scale encaustic murals on stone walls today, though artists like Diego Rivera used the medium for some large public art projects. If I were to do a mural, I would start with a cold wax wall preparation and then move over to hot wax. And maybe back and forth too. I like both.

Encaustic purists will tell you that cold wax is not encaustic because it doesn't require heat. But cold wax can be encaustic if used in an encaustic process. Like hot wax encaustic, cold wax can be fused effectively with heat too. But most important of all is that cold wax is encaustic if you say it is. The cold vs. hot wax issue is tricky, and I invite you to make up your own mind.

Here are a few examples of cold wax applications:

- Creating a ground for supports;
- Intarsia (inlay);
- Underpainting, when a more painterly approach is desired;
- Very thin washes of color on flexible supports such as stretched canvas or paper.

Cold Wax Paste

Wax can be emulsified, that is, turned from a solid to a liquid or paste by combining it with solvents like mineral spirits, turpentine or damar varnish. The proportion of wax pellets or wax medium to solvent is shown in the following recipe:

Easy Cold Wax Paste

- 4-5 parts mineral spirits, damar varnish or turpentine (Taylor, p. 135)
- 4-5 parts beeswax

Place wax and spirits in a glass jar and seal tightly. Shake the jar until wax is coated, and shake the jar daily until the spirits are absorbed and the wax has become a soft paste or gel. This process will take a week to ten days. When finished, you should be able to spoon it out like mayonnaise.

Solvents for cold wax paste

Mineral spirits

Mineral spirits yield a solid white paste after a week. This version of cold wax paint is probably the most cost-effective for priming panels. It supersaturates your wooden boards in a way that traditional gesso can't. When used as the basis for paint, the wax dissolved in mineral spirits can be chalky and dull. Sometimes, that's what you want. For a silkier, translucent cold wax paste, use a damar varnish solvent.

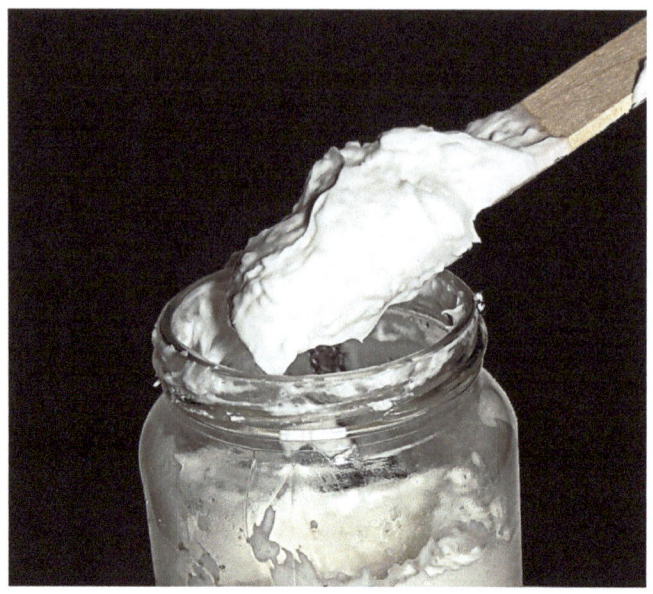

A jar of two-week old cold wax paste made with mineral spirits. This stuff is course and chalky, a good material for priming boards but not great for making paint.

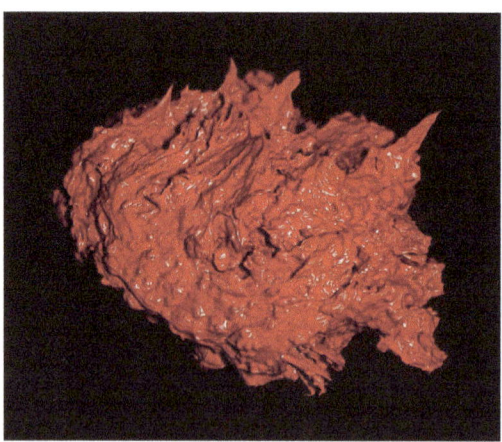

Here is a dab of cold wax paint made with mineral spirits and dry pigment. The finished surface remains chalky and dull.

Damar varnish

Damar varnish is turpentine with damar resin crystals dissolved into it. For an expensive product, it is very simple to make at home—see the **Paint Additives** chapter to learn how. I prefer to use damar varnish as a basis for cold wax paint because it contains many of the superior qualities of damar resin.

Cold wax paint is ready to use after a week, but it seems to get silkier over time. When made according to the proportions above, it yields a thick, translucent, butter-like substance.

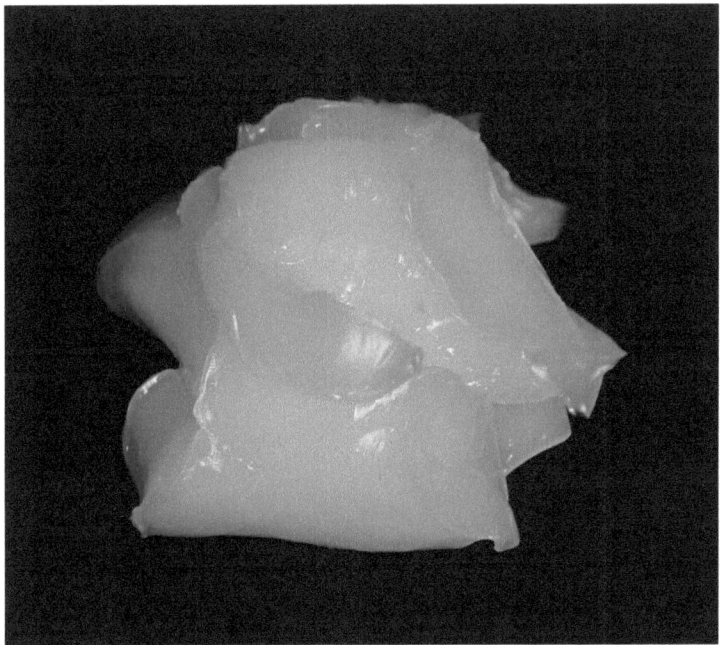

Two week-old cold wax paste made with damar varnish (damar crystals dissolved in turpentine). This is a smooth, translucent gel, a great a basis for paint. It can also be used by itself as a glaze.

Cold Wax Paint

Refer back to **Easy Cold Wax Paste** (previous pages) for the basic cold wax paste recipe. In making cold wax paint, you will be using damar varnish as a solvent.

Working with cold wax paint is nothing like encaustic paint. It can take up to a week to dry (often longer) and the final cured surface can seem dull or even chalky depending on the solvent and additives you used. Mineral spirits, for instance, are not suitable for paint unless a chalky finish is what you want.

However, cold wax paint has some real advantages over hot wax simply because it remains in a liquid state longer and you can do more painterly things with it. It can also go where hot wax won't go—filling narrow channels and pits in wax surfaces without the time-consuming excavation of intarsia.

Tube oil in cold wax paint

Place the desired amount of cold wax medium in a glass jar. Squeeze a small amount of oil paint into the medium and blend, adding more paint until you get the color you want. Don't worry about slaking the paint before hand—you want to have the extra oil. Blend with a spoon or craft stick. When not in use, seal the jar to keep the paint wet and fresh. The paint will have the consistency of mayonnaise; if you need to thin it, add a few drops of turpentine.

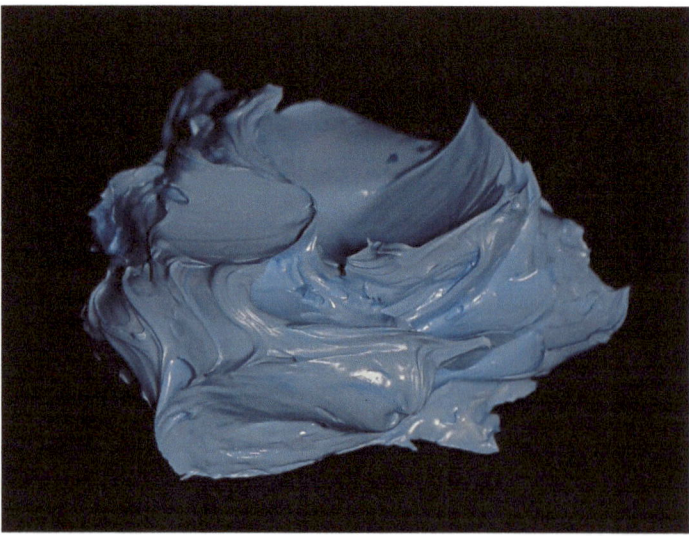

Cold wax paint really is this pretty. The solvent is damar varnish and the color is ultramarine oil paint.

Dry pigment in cold wax paint

Note: Read the chapter on the **Toxicity of Art Materials** to learn safe techniques for handling dry pigment.

Place the desired amount of cold wax medium in a jar and set aside. In your mixing tray, add equal parts dry pigment and linseed oil or stand oil. Blend well, using a craft stick to break up lumps of pigment. Add more oil until mixture is smooth. Add pigment to cold wax medium and blend well. At this point, your paint should look glossy and have the consistency of mayonnaise. Feel free to add more linseed oil or damar varnish. Seal tightly when not in use.

Cold Wax Glaze

There are several formulas for cold wax glaze. Read the chapter on **Colors, Paints and Glazes** for more information.

Cold Wax Saturated Boards and Stone

Once I learned about the ancient Greeks and their mural walls, I decided to prepare some boards and tiles with cold wax medium. Cold wax saturation creates one of the most stable wood-wax bonds, and greatly reduces pin holes and bubbles from your paintings.

Note: Cold wax medium contains volatile solvents which will evaporate when exposed to air and ignite when exposed to flame. Please don't use your butane torch to fuse cold wax medium, and be careful of overheating with your other tools. Once the solvent has gassed off, cold wax medium is as safe as beeswax medium. Please read the instructions for the solvent you used to create the cold wax.

You will need:

- Clean wood panel or stone tile
- Heat gun (do not use a torch)
- Easy cold wax paste
- Paint brush

Step one: Using your heat gun on medium, heat a 6" x6" section of your panel until it is almost too hot to touch.

Step two: Apply a teaspoon or so of paste to the heated section. It will melt like butter and soak into the wood. You may notice some fizzing as air leaves the board. This is what you want. Air inside the board is being replaced by wax. When you use the board later for an encaustic painting, you will notice fewer pinholes and bubbles.

Step three: Repeat steps one and two until surface is covered. At this point the wood will look wet. Only a small amount of wax has penetrated the board at this point. You will need to repeat this process several times to drive out the air.

Step four: I like to let the board rest for a few minutes between applications. I am generally prepping several boards at a time, so I simply add a coat to each board and move on to the next. I have added as many as seven applications of cold wax before the board is saturated, but generally, three applications is enough. You'll know it's done when the hot paste pools on the surface and the air is no longer fizzing out of the board.

When it's cooled you should still be able to feel some of the wood grain with your fingertips, but the surface will be waxy. If you turn the board on edge you might be able to see how deeply the wax penetrated.

When you reheat the surface later, some additional fizzing will occur as wax bubbles out of the wood. This is good. The wax in the wood will fuse and bind with the wax you paint on the surface. There is no need for other gesso compounds.

Advantages: By submitting the board to repeated high heat and infusions of wax paste, most of the gas is driven out of the wood. You should get fewer gas bubbles and pin holes as you paint with encaustics and reheat. Saturating the board with wax creates a very durable wax-wood bond, probably the most stable ground for encaustic.

Disadvantages: The luminosity thing. You still need to add white base layers to the surface if you want that inner glow. Melt a tin of regular wax medium and add a teaspoon of titanium white to create an opaque white paint. Use this as your first base layer of hot wax.

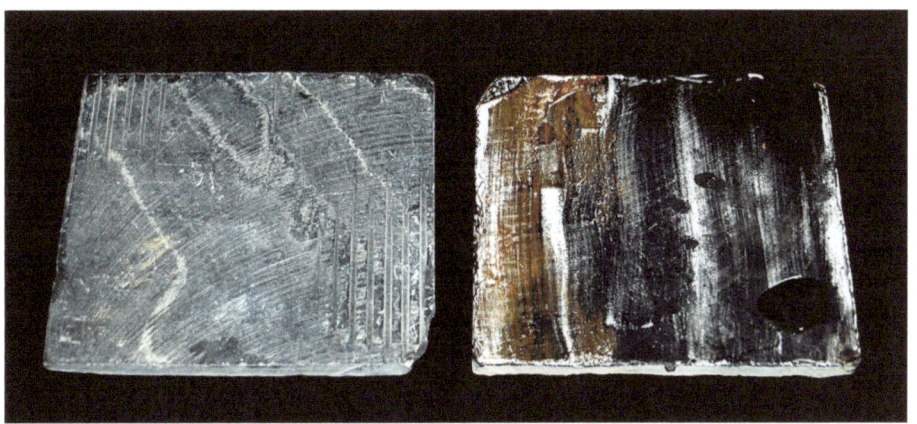

Cold wax saturated... slate. On the left is an untreated piece of slate tile. On the right is tile with six or seven coats of cold wax medium. The stone soaked up the medium, leaving a waxy surface for a hot or cold encaustic painting. The yellow in the tile on the right is a natural color variation of the stone and the white streaks are wax.

Grounds for Encaustic Paintings

Choosing your ground

The beauty of encaustic materials is that you really don't need to do much more than lay down a few coats of plain wax or wax medium to your surface before painting. Nothing is longer-lasting than wax fused to wood. The painters of the Fayum mummy portraits were interested in preserving a living image for all time. With encaustic materials on wooden panels, they have nearly done so. In fact, panel edges and borders, where the ancient artists left the wood bare, the wood fibers are worn and fragile. Where there is wax, the wood is still strong and preserved.

If you don't have to, why prime your supports?

There are several good reasons to take the time to create an intermediary layer—called a ground or priming layer (primer)—between the support and your painting:

- **Stability and archival standards.** Not all supports are created equal. Modern wood products, such as Masonite, continue to release gases from their manufacture for many years, and as such aren't considered archival. Having an absorbent ground between your work and the support is a good idea if you're not sure where the wood came from.

- **Surface texture.** Not all wood panels are created equal, but with a priming layer you can get a perfectly even surface. When primed with certain materials, such as gesso, chalk ground, clay, even joint compound, the artist can fill surface imperfections and sand it to a satin finish. Or the artist can build texture with gesso that will add to impasto effects, if desired.

- **Luminosity.** The inner glow of a beautiful encaustic painting doesn't happen by accident. Primer layers are often white (although they don't have to be). A layer of white gesso at the base of your painting acts like an inner light source.

All of the reasons I give above are good ones for priming your supports, but the best reason of all is because you want to. You know it works with your tools. You don't have to wonder how it will perform. You like how it looks.

Terms to know:

Support. A support is the foundation, panel or backing of your encaustic painting. Almost any rigid material can be used as a support including wood, wall board, even glass, Plexiglas and metal.

Ground. A ground is the actual surface on which you paint. Sometimes called a primer or priming layer, it is the substance that the artist applies to the surface of the support to make it ready to receive paint. Usually, a ground is composed of a binder (glue), an inert filler (chalk) and dry pigment. This chapter will offer a number of different ideas for grounds.

Gesso. Gesso is a traditional kind of ground made to exacting standards. Rabbit-skin glue is the most common binder. It's usually a fairly brittle material when dry and works best with a rigid support.

Grounds and gesso

When I first started out, I was entranced by those virginal white encaustic boards at the art supply store. They are so silky and luminous. I decided a white ground had to be the secret behind all those beautiful encaustic paintings.

But then I checked out the unit cost on those panels. Too expensive, especially if I wanted to make a big piece. All right, so what if I made the panels (or, let's get real here, got my boyfriend to make them) and primed them myself? A couple of encaustic materials manufacturers have great dry and pre-mixed gesso compounds. Then I got a look at *those* prices.

I said I was cheap, right? This is how cheap: I decided to make my own ground. Here is a list of DIY grounds and primers that work, some extremely inexpensive, some more costly.

Like other aspects of this lovely art form, there are dozens of ways to prepare your painting surface, and none is necessarily more correct than any other. You will discover that some methods work better for certain kinds of projects and techniques, and you may decide that having a gallon of pre-mixed gesso or a stack of ready-to-use boards is entirely worth it.

Following is a list of grounds or gesso you can buy or make at home.

Encaustic boards from the art supply store

I know what I said earlier, but to be honest, I love having a few store-bought boards around. They're so easy. Ampersand makes both clay boards (multi-media boards) and encaustic boards primed with R & F Handmade Paint gesso compound. They come in any size from little trading card-sized boards up to 30" x 30". All have a luminous white surface that suffuses your painting with light. These boards are costly but you can always scrape off the wax and start again.

Advantages: Store-bought boards are beautifully finished and ready to go. Remember to preheat the boards with your heat gun for about 30 seconds before adding your first layer of wax.

Disadvantages: It is very easy to incise through layers of wax medium right down to the gesso. Build up sufficient layers of wax before using a sharp tool. On the other hand, some artists use these boards in order to incise through the gesso. Once again, it's all about what works for you.

Beeswax

I mentioned earlier that simply coating your boards or supports with beeswax or beeswax medium is the simplest priming method for encaustic art. I love to use plain yellow beeswax because there is usually some residual honey content. It smells wonderful and feels sticky--both good omens for priming layers!

You will need:

- Plain beeswax or beeswax medium melted on your palette
- Clean, dry board or support

- 3" hake brush
- Heat gun

Step one: Preheat your board using your heat gun. A torch can be used but a heat gun much more effectively spreads the heat.

Step two: Paint melted wax on your board, sweeping the brush evenly, left to right. Because the board is preheated, you should see the wax penetrate slightly into the wood.

Step three: Lightly fuse with your heat gun, sweeping left to right to create an even surface.

Step four: When the board has cooled, check the wax surface to make sure the wax is evenly distributed. Repeat if there are any bare spots.

Pre-Mixed Grounds and Gesso

Chalkboard Paint

I primed my first homemade encaustic boards with Rust-Oleum chalkboard paint. It makes a wonderful surface for wax—toothy yet very smooth. You can get it in black or mix your own color. The black is perfectly dark and velvety. I stopped using it because it's an acrylic-based paint and doesn't really stand up to a lot of heat. You can buy the Rust-Oleum product or make your own using your own paint and non-sanded tile grout. (Pistrucci Artworks)

Encaustic gesso

R & F Handmade Paint makes a nearly perfect gesso for encaustic. The ready-to-use gesso ranges in price from $29 per pound (16-ounce jar) to $14 per pound for an eight-pound tub. R&F also offers a dry gesso compound that you mix yourself. It ranges in price from $14 per pound to $11 per pound for a five-pound bag. At this rate the pre-mix dry compound costs no more than traditional gesso.

Evans Encaustics offers their Holy Grail ready-to-use gesso for $18 per pound (16-ounce jar) to $16 per pound for a 32-ounce tub. Holy Grail comes in a dizzying number of colors. So far, Evans isn't offering a dry version, but they make up for it with sheer ingenuity.

Traditional gesso mix

Traditional gesso is made of a binder like rabbit-skin glue, filler such as chalk, and pigment, usually titanium white. You can buy it ready-to-use or dry to which you add water. If you buy the dry mix, remember to start the recipe the night before you want to use the product. I have to admit, I love to make up a batch and heat it on my palette, imagining myself following the same routine as generations of artists. Gamblin traditional gesso has good, easy-to-follow instructions for use.

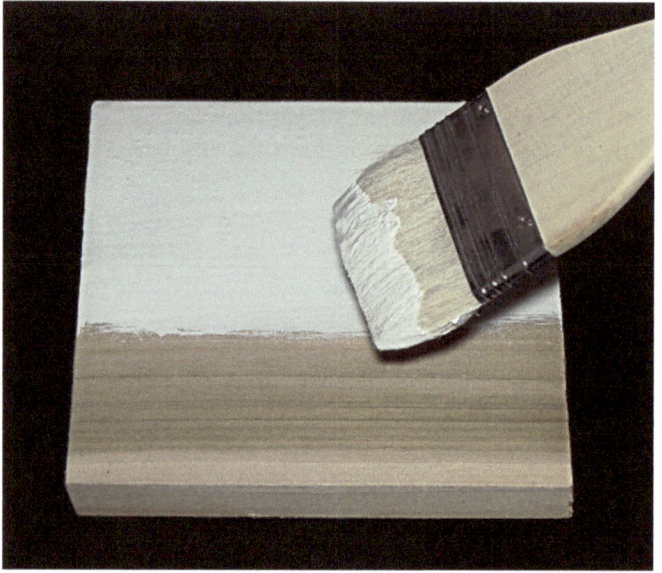

Traditional gesso... smooth, uniform, glistening white perfection.
This why they make the stuff and why we like to use it!

Fillers

If you are going DIY, you need to think about fillers for gesso. The glue or binder that holds the filler together is important, and this chapter includes several recipes using different sorts of binders, but the filler is the body of the gesso, the ground of your painting.

Chalk

Most people use chalk as a filler. Since I live in a rural area, it's been hard to find chalk in a sufficient—and sufficiently cheap—quantity. You can find it online at specialty paint stores like Earth Pigments, but I wanted a lot of it and I wanted it now.

There are other compounds you can use for filler. Some of the common ones I've tried include marble dust and Plaster of Paris. Marble dust is a lovely pure white powder, a component of Venetian plaster. In milk paint preparations, marble dust precipitates out of the solution quickly and glops at the bottom of the bowl. You have to keep mixing as you use it—which you do for all homemade gessos and grounds—but the reward for using marble dust is a finely-grained ground that sands very smooth.

Plaster of Paris

Plaster of Paris is actually gypsum and, according to *Wikipedia*, it got its name from a large gypsum deposit found in Montmartre. (Wikipedia) Aren't you glad you asked? Gypsum is processed with heat, then slaked with water and dried. Commercial Plaster of Paris mixes can be gritty and sandy, often too rough to use as an encaustic ground. When I use PoP (i.e. when the cupboards are bare in the studio), I sift out the larger pieces of stone first. After that, I soak it in water for a few days before using it in a recipe for gesso or ground.

Gypsum

But that's not my last word on gypsum. Gypsum is a soft calcium mineral also known as alabaster. The gypsum we use now is not the same alabaster that the ancient Egyptians, Greeks and Romans used for their vases and statues, though commercial gypsum has a translucent quality very worthy of the name. In the building and home improvement industry, gypsum is the main ingredient in wall board and various kinds of plaster. It's also a good soil amendment, so that's where I went to find it—a well-stocked garden department. It comes in 50-pound bags for $8.

Garden gypsum is a fine, pillowy powder. It's flat white with a faint golden undertone. After my experience with Plaster of Paris, I was expecting it to be rough and sandy, but I found it to be much more like flour. When I started using it, I sifted it and soaked it in water like I did P of P, but it didn't seem to matter. Finally I just sifted it directly into the binder without soaking it first, and I've been using it that way ever since.

Baby powder

And then there's baby powder and talcum. It seems almost too easy, but a pretty good filler for encaustic gesso is right there in your grocery store. Baby powder is composed of cornstarch, fragrance and some other stuff I don't recognize (not talcum), but it actually works. (A.J.'s Arts and Designs) I've tried it in both milk paint gesso and basic chalk ground, and it yields a tight, diaper-fresh gesso. Talcum is slightly toxic and I haven't spent any time trying to locate a cheap supply, but I've heard it works well too.

When I bought two units of baby powder, the grocery clerk gave me a weird look, like "Lady, you're too old to have a baby, you aren't fooling anyone. I know you're a drug queen." Ah, my other, profitable career!

For comparison, a one pound box of Gamblin Traditional Gesso is $17.98, while a pound of home-made gesso with gypsum is $8.76. If you like the silky white surface of classic gesso for your paintings—and you don't mind taking the time to do it—making your own gesso can be very cost effective.

Chalk Ground, homemade

Absolutely nothing is easier than a basic chalk ground. You don't even have to use chalk!

You will need:

- 4 parts white glue, wood glue or archival (ph neutral) hide glue
- 3 parts water
- 4 parts filler (chalk, marble dust, gypsum, Plaster of Paris, baby powder)
- 1 part dry pigment, usually titanium white

Combine water and glue in a large container. In a separate container, combine filler and pigment. Slowly add filler to glue mixture, stirring constantly. Add more filler or water/glue blend to get the consistency you want. Ideally it should be like pancake batter, but you can use a thicker version to build up impasto effects. Read **Appendix C: How to Apply Gesso**.

Rabbit-skin glue
Both *The Painter's Handbook* by Mark David Gottsegen and *The Artist's Handbook* by Ralph Mayer offer gesso formulas that include rabbit-skin

glue. If you want to use this traditional glue, follow the directions on the package. If you use this glue, omit the extra water in the chalk ground recipe above.

Milk paint

Milk paint is another old, old paint formula. In the traditional arts, milk emulsion is used in tempera painting, where the pigment molecule is suspended in milk fat globules, giving the paint a deep, jewel-like clarity. (Mayer, pp. 264-266)

But around the farm, milk paint has a much more work-a-day purpose. It is a homemade, nearly permanent paint that is thousands of years old. Mixed with ochre or other earth minerals, it has been used as both interior and exterior wall paint. In the U.S., farmers made milk paint by the bucket and painted their barns, fences and homes. Google "milk paint" and you'll come up with dozens of sites and recipes. Several companies sell packages of dry milk paint, either plain or with pigment added. View **The Old Fashioned Milk Paint Company** or **The Real Milk Paint Co** (both listed in **Appendix D: Encaustic Supplies**). A package of dry mix that yields a pint of paint costs about $16.95 at either site.

Milk paint penetrates most porous surfaces and it has absolutely no harmful chemicals.

You will need:

- Clean, dry boards or panels
- Milk, regular or powdered
- Hydrated garden lime, available from garden supply centers
- Chalk. You can also use dry joint compound, Plaster of Paris, or gypsum from your garden center
- Sandpaper, medium to fine grades

Basic Milk Paint Recipe

At The Hive Encaustic blog, where our motto is cheap and so is the rest of us, milk paint is a big part of the gesso repertoire. Milk, hydrated lime and gypsum—how do you spell inexpensive? I've championed the original recipe, sometimes called the 1870 Formula, which I found on the **Pioneer Thinking** web site (listed in **Appendix D: Encaustic Supplies**).

You will need:

- 1 quart milk (fresh or powdered and reconstituted)
- 1 ounce hydrated lime (not quick lime)
- 1-2 tablespoons of dry pigment
- 1-2 pounds of filler (chalk, gypsum, marble dust)

If you are using an art-grade hydrated lime or lime putty, add a small amount of milk to the lime to make a creamy paste. . Earth Pigments is a good resource for natural pigments and paint ingredients, including lime and borax. Their web site is listed in **Appendix D: Encaustic Supplies**.

If you are using garden lime (available in most garden centers), you will notice that it has a gritty consistency and is composed of little bits of rock of varying sizes. Try to sieve out the bigger pieces first. Place lime in a small jar and add an equal amount of milk. Seal the jar with a tight lid and shake. Allow the lime and milk to sit half an hour, shaking occasionally. You can't actually dissolve the lime in milk, but you can make sure that the smallest particles of lime are suspended in the milk. After half an hour, pour the mixture through a layer of cheesecloth, reserving the milk and lime mixture and disposing of any little rocks caught in the cheesecloth.

Add the lime to the rest of the milk in a large container and blend well. Stir in your pigment. Place your filler (chalk, gypsum etc.) in a large sieve and sift into the milk mixture. Stir gesso frequently. I've chosen to use gypsum for filler, which is a soft calcium mineral used in plaster and wallboard. I've spent a lot of time sieving and sifting gypsum, even the cheap stuff, and I have never encountered anything except fine, soft powder.

Your paint is finished when it looks like thick, pourable pancake batter. Paint it onto your boards with a gesso brush, using consistent left to right brush strokes. You can stop at one coat or wait until dry to add more coats. Read **Appendix C: How to Apply Gesso.**

By adding more filler (chalk or gypsum), you can build a paste-like paint which you can slather onto your board with a putty knife. This is nice if you want to build up a little more texture under your painting. Thick or thin, milk paint dries leaving a residue of chalk on the surface of the panel which can be sanded smooth.

Advantages: If you like working without a thick layer of gesso between yourself and the support, this paint is for you. The chalky surface is a great primer for wax, and because it soaks deeply into the wood it makes a good permanent bond.

Disadvantages: This is wet paint and it can cause thin boards to warp. You can paint both sides of a board to counter some warping, but it's not always an exact science. Best to use this gesso on braced or cradled boards.

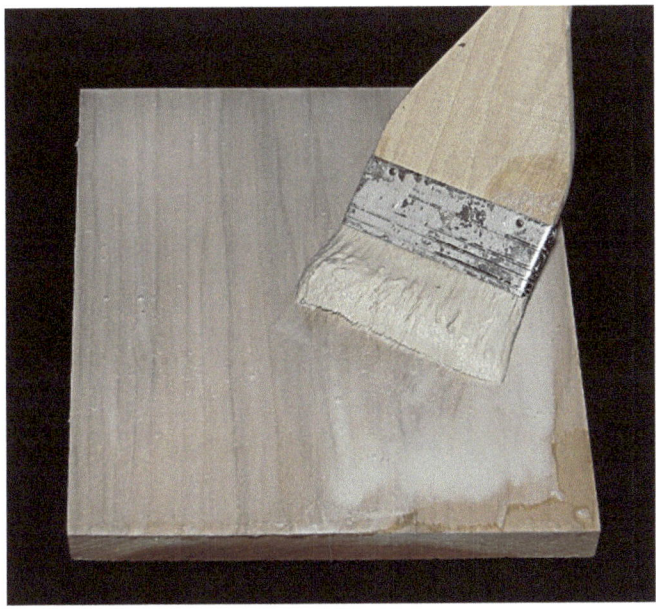

Here I am applying 1870 milk paint as a ground. As you can see, it is wet and thin, though you can bulk it up with more filler. When it is dry, it has a tough, gritty surface.

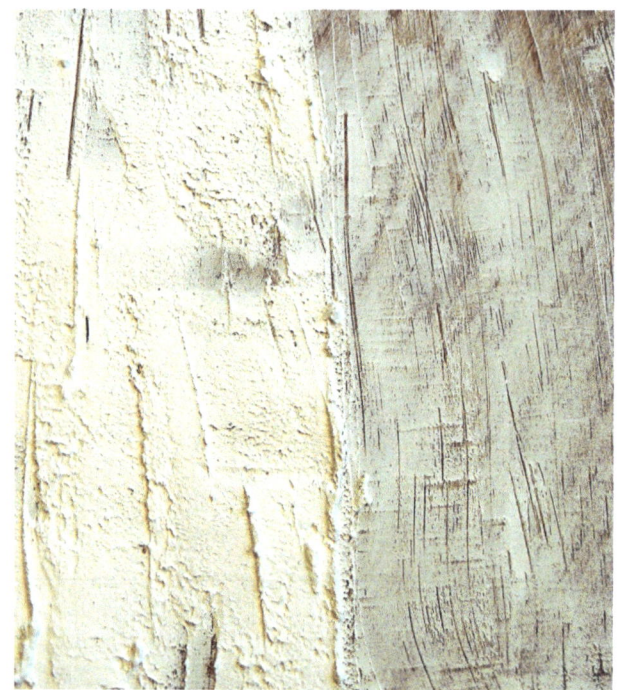

A photo of 1870 recipe milk paint with gypsum filler. On the right is an application of thin paint, on the left the same paint bulked up with much more gypsum to create impasto effects, if desired.

Casein—The Other Milk Paint

Here's another way to make milk paint. It's an old and revered type of homemade paint that utilizes a substance in milk called casein. You can buy dry casein or make your own. The following recipe was adapted from **Earth Pigments Milk and Lime Paint**. As I mentioned in the previous recipe, Earth Pigments is a good resource for natural pigments and paint ingredients, and their web site is listed **in Appendix D: Encaustic Supplies**. For instance, they sell big bags of chalk and very beautifully milled lime, among other things. I recommend you visit the Earth Pigments site and spend some time with their recipes.

You will need:

- 1/2 gallon milk
- 1 cup white vinegar

Have the milk at room temperature before you add the vinegar. Once you add the vinegar stop stirring because the curds are already forming. Let the mixture sit in a warm place overnight. The next day, line a colander with cheesecloth and place it in your sink or over a large bowl. Pour the milk and vinegar mixture through the colander, thus separating the curds from the whey. I don't know what to do with whey but it might be good for something. I just let mine go.

Put the dripping wet curds in a large bowl or gesso container. Some sources say to gently wash the vinegar off the curds but my curds were so fragile I didn't bother. In a separate container, place:

- ½ cup hydrated lime
- ¾ cup water, <u>slowly</u> added to the lime

You should be able to make a creamy paste, though I use garden lime which has to be sifted to remove larger chunks of rock and didn't get anywhere near creamy. This milk paint recipe seems to require a very fine grade of lime, which you might want to buy specially. The 1870 milk paint recipe isn't nearly as finicky.

Add the lime/water combination to the curds and stir. The curds should start to break down and become smooth. If this doesn't happen, you can add:

- ½ teaspoon of borax

When the curds are smooth and the paint resembles pancake batter, add:

- 1-2 tablespoons of dry pigment
- 3-4 cups of filler such as chalk, gypsum, even baby powder

Blend until it is smooth and luscious, and add more filler until you get the consistency you want. Use a gesso brush to paint your boards, making nice, even left to right strokes. Allow to dry overnight and add another coat, if desired. Read Appendix C: How to Apply Gesso. When the gesso is thoroughly dry, sand it until silky.

My version of casein milk paint gesso still had a few lumpy curds. Next time I will probably run it through the food processor. But when fully dry, the gesso is solid and tight and easy to sand. I have to say I still prefer the 1870 version for sheer simplicity, but this paint is nice and if I ever want to distress any furniture, I know where to go.

Canvas

Canvas, stretched

The natural flex in large stretched canvas isn't good for thick layers of wax but sometimes canvas is just what you want. For hot wax, you can get nice effects with small stretched practice canvases. Try sizes no larger than 8" x 8" and be sure to get canvases prepared for oils. Acrylic gesso melts under heat.

For larger canvases, there are cold wax formulas that work as well as oil paint. Read the chapter on **Colors, Paints and Glazes** for more information. Some artists use wax emulsions that are thinned with turpentine or oil to the point where the colors can be brushed on like watercolor.

Canvas mounted on board

Canvas is a perfect support for wax because it is highly absorbent. If you want to work on canvas, you can create rigid panels or boards mounted with canvas.

Step one: Cut a piece of canvas duck or linen to the shape of your board, leaving two extra inches of margin on each edge.

Step two: Brush the surface of your board with archival glue or rabbit skin glue. Place the canvas square over the board and press the canvas down, smoothing from the center to the edges to remove any wrinkles. Turn it over, board side up, and weight with a heavy object. When the glue is set and the canvas feels dry and secure, wrap the edges of the canvas around the back of the board and glue them down. Weight and allow to dry, as before.

Step three: Turn the board face up. Warm the canvas with your heat gun and apply hot melted wax (either plain wax or medium), making sure to saturated the canvas all the way to the board. Allow to fully cool, at least several hours.

Canvas, wax-saturated

I fell in love with the description of Victor Brauner's experiments with wax-saturated canvas, as told in *Encaustic Materials and Methods* by Francis Pratt and Becca Fizell (Pratt, pp. 37-38). A Romanian Surrealist and communist, Brauner was forcibly isolated in the Alps during World War II, where it was hard to get his usual art materials. During this time he developed a method of saturating unstretched canvas panels with a thick layer of melted beeswax. He then etched into the surface with a sharp tool and washed the surface with a glaze of black oil paint mixed with something called *essence of gasoline*. Whatever the substance, it was volatile and evaporated quickly. (And no, I haven't tried this.) He then washed the surface with gasoline again so that only the black incised lines remained.

Making a wax-saturated canvas board is simple, and the result is a remarkably rigid (though fragile) support for encaustic.

You will need:

- Squares of fairly thick canvas duck or linen
- Raw, unbleached beeswax
- Palette heated to 200 degrees F
- Hake brush, heat gun
- Waxed paper

Step one: Melt beeswax until it is thin and liquid. Watch your temperature to not overheat.

Step two: I started with 6" x 8" squares of linen and determined which side would be front and which side back. Place linen back-side up on a sheet of clean waxed paper. Using your heat gun on a high setting, holding it six inches from canvas, heat the whole area with smooth even strokes, about 30 seconds.

Step three: Brush on a layer of melted beeswax. Try to cover the entire area but don't worry if it dries very quickly.

Step four: Using your heat gun, heat the surface until the wax melts and fully penetrates the fibers of the canvas. It should look wet. Allow to cool lying flat. When fully cool, don't be surprised if the wax paper has stuck to your work surface and the canvas has stuck to the wax paper. Use your heat gun to loosen it up. Turn the canvas over, front side up.

Step five: Now you will add three layers of wax, cooling well after each application. For the first layer, heat the canvas until it looks wet. Apply a layer of wax, brush strokes going in one direction. Fuse heavily, allowing this layer to penetrate the fibers. Cool. Turn the canvas 90 degrees to the right so that your brush strokes go in a different direction. Apply another layer of wax and fuse, but this time using your heat gun's medium setting. Fuse until this layer is shiny but not liquid.

Step six: Your canvas may look lumpy at this point, the wax a thick yellow layer obscuring the canvas underneath. Use your iron to fuse the top layer again, smoothing the surface flat. Wait a couple of hours so that the entire piece is quite cool and iron the surface again.

This is a time consuming process. I try to do three squares at a time so that I can work on the second piece as the first cools.

Advantages: This process creates a thick bed of wax that is perfect for deep incising and drawing. The pieces are rough, and the final look is nothing like an ultra-clean Ampersand cradled panel. But you can get some wonderful effects by allowing the fabric to show through.

Disadvantages: Even if you use bleached white beeswax the look of the wax-canvas boards will be rustic. Because the boards will always be a fragile and prone to flex, consider framing your finished piece in a box.

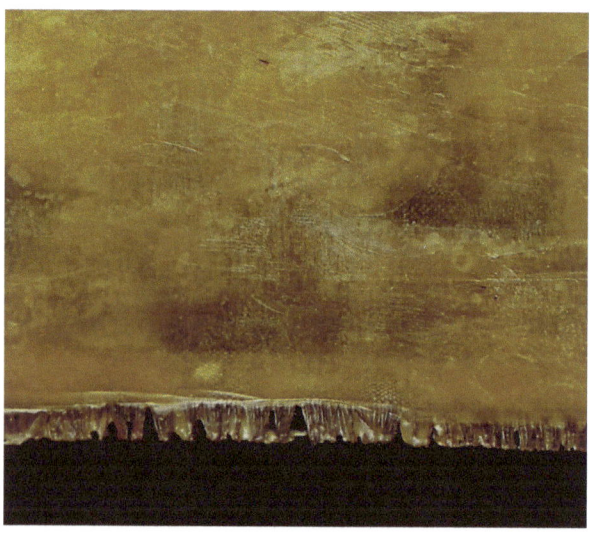

Wax-saturated linen from the front.

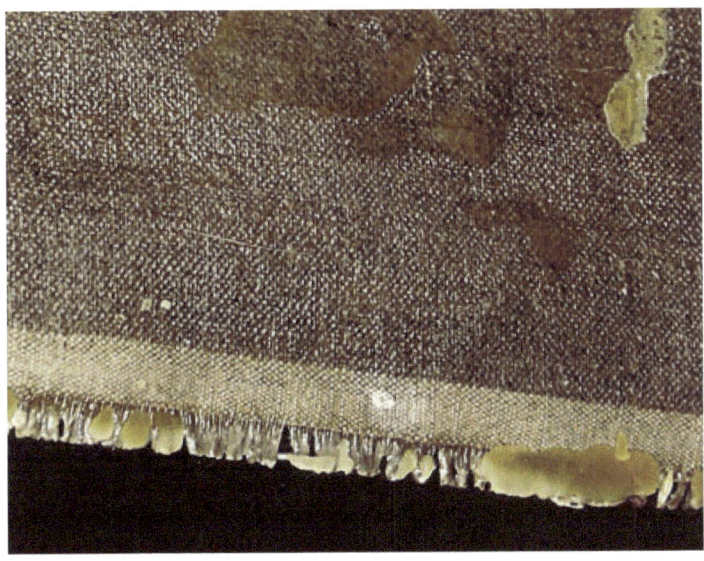

Wax-saturated linen from the back.

Drywall joint compound

Pre-mixed drywall joint compound is cheap, easy to use, white and creamy-smooth. It's available seven days a week at your favorite hardware store. It's made of lime, perlite, clay and various chemical polymers, some of which may react unpredictably under heat. You just never know. Joint compound can be a great way to get started, but remember that it is a brittle material. Tape the edges of your support with masking tape to prevent bumping and cracking.

You will need:

- Clean, dry board
- Container of drywall joint compound, sometimes called mud
- Putty knife
- Package of sandpaper, medium to fine grades

Buy several metal putty knives of different widths, such as a 1", 2" and 4". You'll find the putty knives in your hardware store, either in the paint department or right next to tubs of joint compound. Plastic putty knives are cheaper but consider splurging on metal knives because they are so useful around the encaustic studio. Scoop out several tablespoon of the grayish compound and spread evenly over the surface of the board to a thickness of

1/32" to 1/16". You can add as many coats as you want, but try to keep them thin.

For best results, smooth the compound in one direction only; don't use random strokes. Read **Appendix C: How to Apply Gesso**.

Now the compound needs to dry, and I mean really *dry*. This may take anywhere from a few hours to overnight. As it dries it will turn white. After the board is dry, use medium to fine grade sandpaper and go over the surface lightly. Remember, joint compound is soft. It's all too easy to sand right through it to the wood below. If you'd like, apply a second thin coat and dry and sand as before. Don't worry about sanding it too smooth because you want some tooth on the surface to absorb the wax and make that permanent bond.

Advantages: This is a cheap and reliable ground for encaustic supports. And it is comparatively fast. It's good for rigid panels but not suitable for canvas or anything wobbly. This product was designed for walls, after all.

Disadvantages: If applied too thickly, dried compound may crack and fall away, especially near the edges of the board. Support the edges with masking tape and saturate the entire surface with wax or wax medium, heating the surface gently to maximize absorption.

Cold wax saturated boards

Cold wax saturation creates one of the most stable wood-wax bonds, and greatly reduces the occurrence of pin holes and bubbles in your paintings. I discussed it earlier in the **Cold Wax for Encaustic** chapter, but if you missed it, go back and read it. Cold wax medium is a great way to prepare wood and stone surfaces and has been used since ancient times

Advantages: By submitting the board to repeated high heat and infusions of wax paste, most of the gas is driven out of the wood. You should get fewer gas bubbles and pin holes as you paint with encaustic and reheat. Saturating the board with wax creates a very durable wax-wood bond, probably the most stable ground for encaustic.

Disadvantages: The luminosity thing. You still need to add white base layers to the surface if you want that inner glow. Melt a tin of regular wax medium and add a teaspoon of titanium white to create an opaque white paint. Use this as your first base layer of hot wax after prepping your board with cold wax.

Watercolor paper

I love this preparation method for small boards. It satisfies my wrapping-paper fetish, plus the backs of the panel are really tidy and neat. Paper is also one of the best grounds for wax.

You will need:

- Watercolor paper. You want lush, toothy paper but it has to be foldable. Not too thick. Higher grades of paper soak up the wax like hungry earth, so spend a little more to get good stuff.
- Archival, pH neutral glue
- Clean board
- Scissors, brush

Step one: Cut the paper in the shape of the board, leaving 2" to 3" margin all around.

Step two: Apply the glue to one side of the board with a clean brush. The glue should be spread evenly; if it's too thick, thin it with a little water.

Step three: Place the paper over the board. Smooth surface with your fingertips, working from the center of the board and pressing out all the air bubbles.

Step four: Weight the board with a heavy book or other object for several hours until the glue is set.

Step five: When the boards are dry, turn paper-side down and fold and glue the extra paper around the edge and over the back, like a birthday present. I usually notch the corners of the paper to make it lie flat. Weight the board for several hours until the glue is set

Step six: Apply a base coat of wax medium to the front surface. Preheat the papered board by gently sweeping the surface with your heat gun, being careful not to overheat. Paper is already a very absorbent support and pre-heating is more of a suggestion here. Brush on a base coat of hot wax medium. Fuse with an iron to cement the paper fully to the board.

Advantages: Paper creates a smooth, warm surface. Hot wax loves paper and it works especially well with heat gun and iron. The finished painting makes a nice gift.

Disadvantages: Paper grounds are not ideal for heavy incising. Also gluing and drying the boards takes some time. I often prepare ten boards at a go so that I have a stack in reserve.

Colors, Paints and Glazes

Color

Human history has been devoted to the creation of colored paint (among a few other things). The colors we use were developed over thousands of years from both organic and inorganic substances. Some colors are made from plants and animals, others from minerals and earth. Many colors are now synthesized in labs. One characteristic shared by all pigments is that they are insoluble—they don't dissolve or break down into their component parts in water or oil, though many will fade or discolor over time.

My advice: Be fearless where color is concerned. Don't be afraid to make mud. Dry pigments and tube oils come in every color, and you can add them to your wax medium in any amount or saturation. The trick is to remember what you did the *next time* you want to use that color.

This is not a small consideration, especially for those of us who don't get out to the studio very often. Take blue, for instance. I wanted to match a blue I used in an older piece, a blue that came out of someone's old tube of oil paint. I remember that after I had squished out every drop, I tossed the tube and forgot the name of the color. Fast forward two years. I came across the piece of art and remembered how much I liked that blue. It was very like a standard blue, except there was a little ultramarine in it. I thought maybe that old tube had been Prussian blue, thinned out in wax medium but I couldn't remember.

But when I bought both dry pigment and tube oils with those names, I realized how wrong I was. My blue was clearer than Pthalo, lighter than Prussian, not so chemically intense as ultramarine. But then, there was the question of wax. Had I mixed it with white or yellow wax? Had I mixed it with anything else, like linseed oil or turpentine?

This is exactly why pre-mixed encaustic paints were invented. For the most part, you can buy a color from a reliable manufacturer a month or a year later and the batches will be nearly the same. Manufacturers like Enkaustikos, Evans, Miles Conrad or R&F offer rainbows of color sticks and encaustic paint. Etsy and eBay also offer homemade medium and paints by other artists.

Keep in mind that slight color variations can happen even in the factory, under the most controlled situations. And after it enters your studio? Look out for splashes, accidental brush dips and other impurities.

The best control in this bouquet of possibilities is you. Label your paints when you make them and create a detailed color chart.

Color chart

For the longest time, I thought creating a color chart was a waste of time. I would remember what that blue was, right? Wrong. I didn't remember. And, let's be honest, at my age, I will never remember.

Get a spiral-bound sketch book of thick watercolor paper, and before entering anything, consider what you'd like to track in your color book. If you want some ideas, open any art supply catalog and flip to the paint section. You will see sample color swatches for each color. But you will need more information for your chart. Here is what I track in my color book:

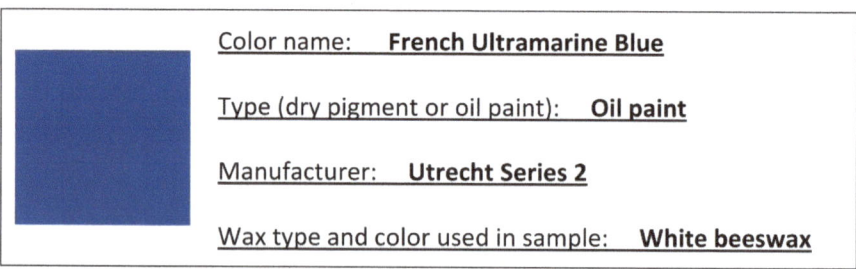

With this information I can recreate the color—or get pretty close. You can organize your book by color and type, and other artists will be amazed at your self-discipline. No splashing around and random dripping for you!

Making Colors

Oil paint

Using a metal paint mixing tray, add a dab of each color oil paint to each well. Spoon some melted wax into each well. Place the tray on your heated palette and using a craft stick, paint brush or cotton swab, mix the paint. View your color under natural light, adjust with more wax or more paint. Dab colors into your color chart and make notes.

Dry pigment

Note: Please take all precautions when mixing dry pigments (use gloves and ventilated face mask). No matter how careful you are, pigment will get everywhere. For more information, read the chapter called **Toxicity of Art Materials.**

Add a half teaspoon of dry pigment to each well of your metal mixing tray. Follow it with a half teaspoon of linseed oil. Blend with a cotton swab, paint brush or craft stick. Once the pigment is fully saturated with oil, it is as safe as oil paint (which is to say, slightly less hazardous). Add melted wax medium, moving the tray to your heated palette. When warmed, test your color and add notes to your chart.

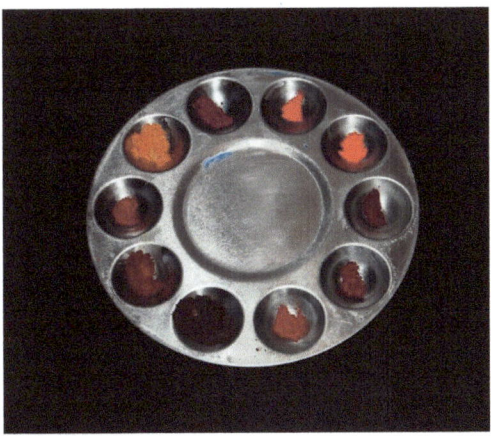

Metal mixing tray full of dry pigment powder. Can you tell the difference between natural red oxides and colors made with cadmium?

Labeling your paint

Say you are more free-spirited and you just want to try one little color experiment. Keep a supply of wooden craft sticks on your work table and as you create a new color, write the pigment and wax type on the stick in Sharpie pen. Use the stick to stir the paint and leave it in the container. Whenever you come back, there's your tin of neatly labeled paint. This will improve your studio experience immeasurably, and you'll be cool.

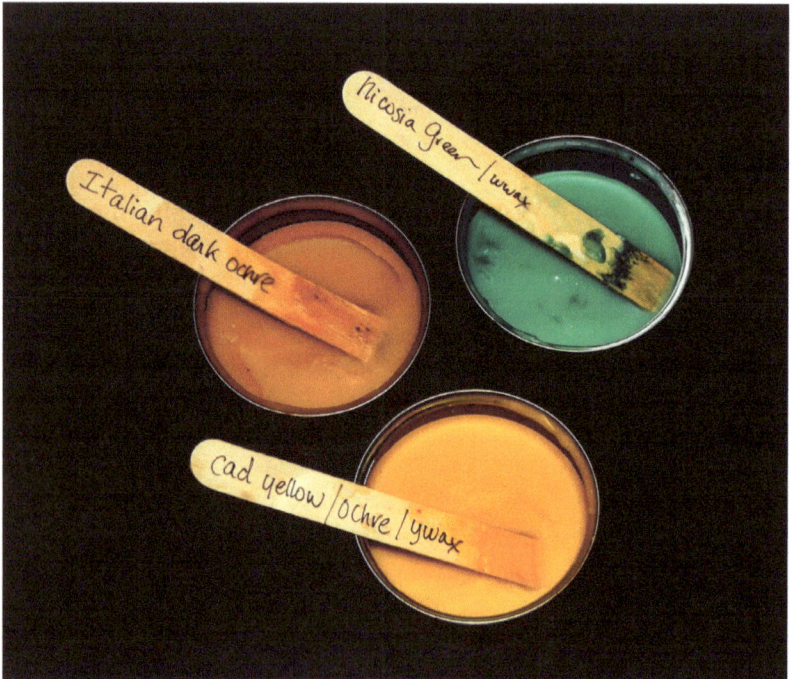

Nicely labelled cans of cold wax. Except for one--I forgot to record what kind of wax was used to create the Italian dark ochre. Darn!

Making Encaustic Paint

Color is an immense topic involving the study of optics as well as a deep knowledge of pigment, medium and binders. Colors appear differently in different media. For instance, encaustic paint is made of pigment particles suspended in wax which gives encaustic paintings their depth and luminosity. Tempera paint is said to glow in much the same way as encaustic, by virtue of the tiny globs of pigment suspended in the fatty mixture of egg or milk.

When you look at a work of art, ask yourself where the color sits on the paper or canvas. Watercolor seeps into a thick porous mat of paper. Acrylic and oil paint ride on top of the support, as does encaustic. Can you look into the paint? Or is the paint flat like a poster or sign?

In its most basic form, encaustic paint is medium + pigment, heated to a brushable liquid. But the kind of pigment you use, whether from oil paint or dry powder, impacts the clarity and drying time of the paint you create. Even pre-made cakes of encaustic paint can vary a great deal from color to color depending on the composition of the pigment (whether organic or inorganic) and the amount of pigment that is needed to express the color.

If you are making your own paint, there are two ways to get pigment into your wax:

1. --Use tube oil paint (never acrylic).
2. --Use dry pigment powder mixed with a little linseed oil.

Oil paint in a tube

You can find oil paint at any art supply or craft store, in many eye-popping colors. I recommend starting with a small set of basic colors. An eight tube set including white and black is all you need to start.

You will need:

- Oil paint
- Paper towel
- 5 oz tin of melted wax medium
- Stir stick

Step one: <u>Slaking</u>. Squeeze a small amount of oil paint onto a paper towel and let sit overnight. The paper towel will leech excess oil from the paint. Some paint types will release a lot of oil. Generally, higher quality paint has more pigment and less oil. Too much oil can make the wax flexible and slower to dry.

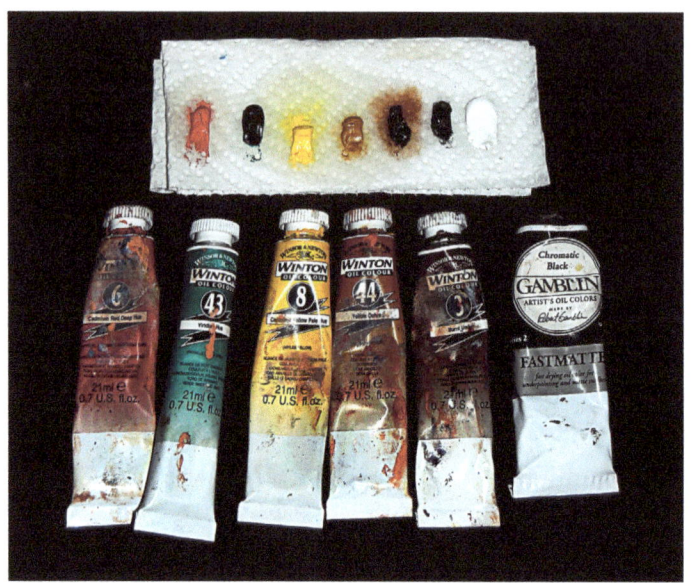

Some oil paints can have a lot of oil in them, as you can tell from this photo. More oil in your encaustic paint can slow drying time.

Step two: Using a stir stick, palette knife or metal spoon, add a small dab of slaked paint to the melted medium and stir well. Test the color on an absorbent sheet of paper, adding more paint until you get the shade you want.

Note: If you are unsure about the color, carry the test paper outside and view in natural light. It helps, especially if you are working under fluorescent light in your studio.

As you paint, you will notice that the encaustic paint will cool and harden at a different rate depending on how much oil was in the tube you added to the medium. The pigment itself could also affect the cooling and drying rate—some paints need a lot more pigment than others to create color.

Note: Oil paint, like every other compound in the artist's studio, can be hazardous. Always use latex gloves when handling paint, and remember to cap your tubes and put them away when you are finished.

Once you turn off your palette and the paint cools, it is preserved. No need to cover. Come back in a day, a year, a thousand years, and your paint will reheat and melt into the same glorious color.

Dry pigment

Dry pigment is a finely ground powder. It is quirky and unpredictable, with textures varying widely from color to color. Some dry pigments will always feel sandy or chalky, others will blend smoothly, still others need to be stirred a lot to stay in suspension.

Buy several colors when you start out. You can't tell from the factory catalogue color chart (especially online) what those colors will do when mixed with wax. Creating a color chart (see above) of your own will help you get a feel for the working properties of the compounds, and how much you will need to make your paint.

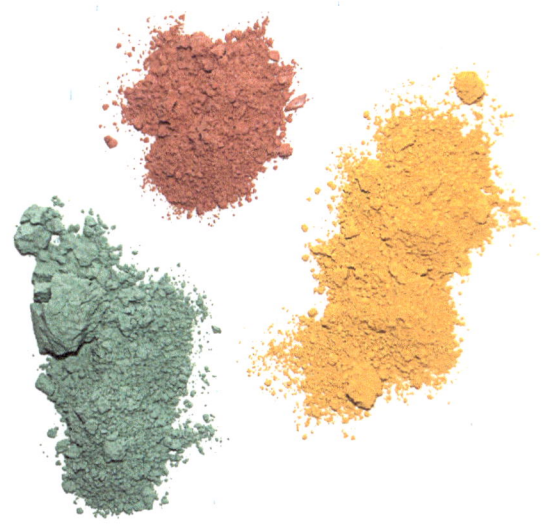

Dry pigments. Nicosia green, pink pipestem and yellow ochre. And yes, I was wearing my mask.

Dry pigment safety tips

Dry pigments are toxic and dangerous. Read Ralph Mayer's extensive chapter on pigments (Mayer, pp. 29-166) and just admit, as I have, that it makes no sense to try to remember which pigments are deadly carcinogens and which are just irritating. Treat them all as if they are nuclear waste. Modern pigments can be made from cobalt, strontium, cadmium, and arsenic, among others. You do not want these compounds to touch you. Since these are often the brightest and prettiest colors, they are probably safer if purchased as oil paints where the oil content renders them nearly harmless, unless you eat the paint or paint your body with it. Don't.

For basic safety, use a face mask respirator, latex gloves, and cover any exposed skin. Safest of all is to use a "chemical glove box" for handling pigments. Search the internet for ready-made units or for instructions to build your own.

You will need:

- Dry pigment powder
- Craft stick
- Round metal paint mixing tray with wells
- Cotton swabs
- Linseed oil
- Tin of melted wax medium

Step one: Place a tin of wax medium on your heated palette to melt.

Step two: Scoop a teaspoon of pigment from the jar and place in a well on your metal paint-mixing tray. This tray should be on your table, not on your heated palette.

Step three: Add a teaspoon of linseed oil to pigment. Using a cotton swab or craft stick, blend and grind the pigment into the oil until you have a thin paste. The oil helps break up any lumps in the powder and allows the pigment to blend with the wax. Add more linseed oil if necessary—you don't want the paste to be too thick. Remember that some pigments will blend effortlessly, while others remain gritty no matter how much oil you add. Too much linseed oil can slow down the drying time, so keep that equation in mind when you mix your paint.

Step four: Discard the cotton swab. Using the stir stick or a brush, add half the pigment mixture to the hot wax tin on your palette. Blend well, being sure to scrape the bottom of the tin in order to fully incorporate the pigment and the wax. Once dry pigment is in wax suspension is about as safe as oil paint. Cooled to a solid cake, it's inert. Nevertheless, you should keep it away from children and pets.

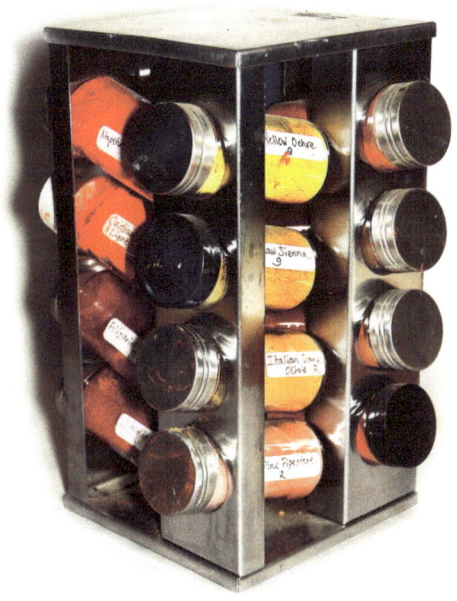

My carousel of color. A very lucky yard sale find.

Encaustic Paint Recipes

Artists have created their own paint recipes over the centuries to accommodate their supports, working styles, and artistic interests. Long before R & F Handmade Paint ever sold their first oil stick, artists were experimenting with hot wax paint and wax emulsion recipes. Frances Pratt and Becca Fizell documented a number of different methods in their 1949 text, *Encaustic Materials and Methods*, and the book remains an invaluable resource.

I became fascinated by *Encaustic Materials and Methods* when every contemporary overview of encaustic art referred to the text--and yet nobody had a copy of it. This was like waving a red flag in front of my nose, and suddenly nothing mattered except possessing this book. I trolled libraries, I set up searches on various used book and auction sites. Months passed. And then one day a copy appeared on Amazon. Think duck on a June bug, think cat pursuing a mouse, think Terminator. I couldn't click fast enough.

When the book arrived, I found it very worth the wait and I set to work trying out a number of the recipes. I have included recipes here that I found the most interesting, with some substitutions and modifications. For instance, natron and copal resin: not available in my neck of the woods.

Some artists interviewed by Pratt and Fizell wanted a medium that was flexible or dried more slowly, like oil paint, while still having the depth and inner glow of encaustic paint. Others used thin cold wax compounds to fill delicate incised lines in wax surfaces. Still others were traditionalists, using only hot wax in their work, or even reviving the recipe documented by Pliny the Elder. (Pratt, pp. 47-48) There were as many ideas as there were artists.

Contemporary artists benefit from standardized products created by encaustic paint manufacturers, such as R & F Handmade Paint, Evans, Enkaustikos and others (links to these sites can be found in **Appendix D: Encaustic Supplies**). These commercial paints are reliable, predictable, safe, and perfectly suited to the tools and methods encaustic artists use today.

But predictability can also limit creativity. In fact, you will find yourself mixing paints almost from the first day, adding a little more yellow to your green to make it pop, thinning out some red to make a glaze. And that's just the beginning. Art is experimentation and exploration, and you should never allow yourself to become imprisoned by the "right" way to do things. Many artists became great by choosing the "wrong" way.

All of the following recipes that contain extra oil, varnish or turpentine will dry and harden differently than commercially available encaustic paint cakes, so adjust your expectations. I have found, however, that softer paints are very good for intarsia or for built-up surface techniques. Fuse with a very light hand as the paint will melt easily until fully cured.

Note: recipes and sources for sun-thickened linseed oil and damar varnish follow in the **Paint Additives** chapter.

Karl Zerbe's Paint

Karl Zerbe (1903-1972) was a major figure in the mid-twentieth century artistic movement called Boston Expressionism. He was head of the Department of Painting at the School of the Museum of Fine Arts in

Boston, and a major force in the revival of encaustic art. Here is Pratt and Fizell's rendering of Zerbe's basic encaustic paint recipe:

"On a cold support, which Zerbe seems to find most satisfying for his own artistic expression, the paint hardens at once--similar to fast-drying tempera technique. This medium renders a good elastic color which may be heated and mixed daily on the palette.... Good quality turpentine is used for thinning and glazing...." (Pratt, pp. 33-34)

You will need:

- 9 parts beeswax
- 1 part sun-thickened linseed oil (see Paint Additives for more information about sun-thickened linseed oil. You can substitute regular linseed oil until you know whether you like this recipe)

Step one: Melt the wax and oil in a large tin on your palette. If using dry pigment, reserve a portion of the oil to blend with the dry substance. In your mixing tray, work the pigment and oil until it is a smooth paste. Mix the pigment into the wax and oil combination.

This paint mixture is slightly more oil-enriched than the basic encaustic paint recipe discussed earlier. As a result, the paint may take several days to fully harden. However, if you are working with intarsia or scraping techniques, this slow-to-harden paint could be your new best friend. As always, keep in mind what you want to do with the material when deciding what recipe to use.

Fusing: Use a light touch when fusing these layers. Hold your heat gun 12 inches above the support and sweep from side to side. Pull away as soon as the surface begins to shine.

Norman Daly's Mixed Wax Paint

Norman Daly (1911-2008) taught at Cornell University for over fifty years. Frances Pratt and Becca Fizell interviewed him for *Encaustic Materials and Methods*, and here is his formula for mixed wax paint: (Pratt, p. 41)

You will need:

- 5 ½ parts beeswax
- 1 part paraffin

- 1 ½ parts sun-thickened linseed oil oil (see the chapter on **Paint Additives** for more information about sun-thickened linseed oil. Substitute regular linseed oil until you know whether you like this recipe)
- 1 part turpentine
- 1 part damar varnish

Step one: Melt beeswax and paraffin together. Because paraffin's melting point is so much lower than beeswax, there is no need to heat the waxes above 150° F.

Step two: Remove from heat and slowly, **carefully** add the volatile substances, starting with the linseed oil. Use dry pigment for color, blending with a little linseed oil before adding to medium. This medium should be used on a rigid support.

Rifka Angel's Mixed Wax Paint

A very flexible formula that does not contain beeswax. (Pratt, pp. 36-37)

You will need:

- 2/3 part synthetic wax (microcrystalline, multiwax, montan)
- 1/3 part candelilla wax
- small piece of paraffin

Angel kept the wax mixture warm and liquid on her gas stove and applied it to her painting with a palette knife. When the painting was completely finished, she burned it in with hot iron over wax paper. Later she would go back in and touch up details with oil paint. When the painting was fully dried, she would burn it in one last time with a hot iron.

Rifka Angel's recipe says that you can use carnauba wax in place of candelilla wax, but if so, increase the amount of synthetic wax to 3/4 part and use 1/4 part carnauba wax.

Esther Geller's Paint

This recipe yields a luscious, glossy paint. In some ways the most painterly of the hot wax paints, it is also the most difficult to work with after it has cooled and because of its high resin content. (Pratt, p. 45)

You will need:

- 1 cake (about ½ cup liquid measure) of Half and Half Encaustic Medium from Wax Medium Recipes.
- ¼ cup stand oil (see Paint Additives for more information)
- ¼ cup turpentine (original recipe calls for Venice turpentine)

Step one: Melt the cake of medium in a paint tin on your palette. When fully liquid, add the stand oil and turpentine.

Step two: If you are coloring the paint with oil paint, add it directly to the wax mixture and blend. If using dry pigment, mix the dry powder with stand oil or turpentine to form a paste, then add it to the wax.

Blend the wax mixture until it reaches the consistency of butter. While in this warm, gooey state, load your brush with paint and enjoy. But as it cools, you will notice that it becomes sticky, pitchy even a little like melted plastic. This paint is not suitable for intarsia or for any techniques that require scraping. It retains a lovely candy-like surface when cool.

Cold Wax Paint

Read the **Cold Wax for Encaustic** chapter for information.

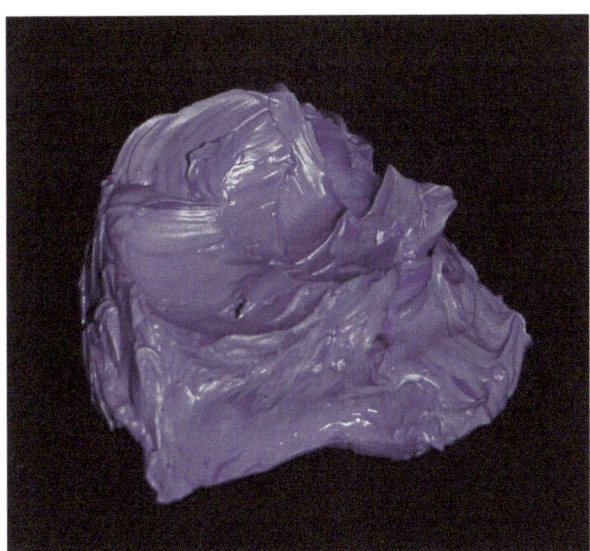

An almost edible image of cold wax paint made with a damar varnish solvent and oil paint.

Glazes

A glaze is a thin, transparent layer of medium added to the surface of a painting. Generally in encaustic, a top layer of clear wax lightly fused is sufficient. You should always try that first if you want a surface treatment. I began to explore glazes when I started to work with both hot and cold wax on the same piece.

While I loved the contrast between the dry matte finish of cold wax and the luminous quality of hot wax, I also wanted a way to see into the painting and identify the different layers. A final layer of clear hot wax was too cloudy and thick for me to see those layers. I settled on a very thin glaze that added no depth or texture to the work, yet acted like a window into the painting itself.

Following are three glaze recipes, two hot wax and one cold. After you scan these recipes, view the glaze comparison chart at the end of this chapter to see the different results.

Half and Half (half beeswax and half damar resin)

For a thick, translucent glaze with more bloom control than regular wax, try the Half and Half encaustic medium recipe in the **Wax Medium Recipes** chapter. When I made a batch of half and half medium and poured it into muffin tins, I noticed that the medium didn't shrink while cooling and it was difficult to release from the pans. It also had a nice, hard gloss. I melted a cake on my palette and used it to glaze a piece where I'd worked some oil paint into the surface.

Glazing: Melt a half and half cake on your palette. Brush the hot liquid onto your painting, trying to minimize lumps and bumps. Fuse lightly with your heat gun. This creates a hard, sticky surface, and scraping will be difficult. Use an iron to even out imperfections and scrape while the wax is warm. I've heard that high-resin content will make wax more brittle. While I haven't noticed this, please experiment before using it on larger pieces.

David Aronson's Hot Glaze

Aronson used the following recipe (Pratt, p. 41) as a glaze for his encaustic paintings. I can't speak for what he was trying to achieve with a final surface treatment but I know that when I use this glaze it has a clarifying and leveling effect on the underlayers, especially if I've used layers of both hot and cold wax.

You will need:

- 1 part damar varnish
- 1 part linseed oil
- 8 parts beeswax

Step one: Place all ingredients in a metal container and heat on your palette. It will melt and blend like all your other encaustic paints, so please be sure to label it.

Glazing: The hot glaze will be very thin and liquid. Dip a putty knife into the glaze and transfer the knife to your piece, scraping down the length of your panel in smooth, even strokes. You want the glaze layer to be as thin as possible. Because the glaze needs to be applied hot, I stood over the palette, holding the panel in my left hand while I quickly dipped and scraped with my right.

The glaze is glossy, so you can see immediately where you've missed spots. Spend some time making sure you have full coverage, and that the glaze layer is as thin as possible. Applied too thickly, it will dry a cloudy white. You can fuse with a heat gun, but do it carefully so that you don't damage the underlayers.

As you can see from the glaze comparison chart at the end of this chapter, drying time for this formula is ridiculous. Expect to wait up to two weeks. But once the surface is no longer tacky to the touch, you can polish it with a microfiber cloth as you would a hot wax piece. The glaze preserves the depth of the underlayers without adding any significant clouding or color.

Fred Conway's Cold Wax Glaze

Fred Conway (1900-1972), like Karl Zerbe, was another mid-century artist and master of encaustic, who was also an important teacher. He was an instructor of painting at the St. Louis School of Fine Arts, Washington University in St. Louis and befriended the German Expressionist Max Beckmann, who painted an extraordinary portrait of his friend. Conway worked in an unusual way, dipping a brush or palette knife into tube oil color, then into hot wax to be applied to prepared surfaces. As he worked, he manipulated the paint by smoothing the paste with turpentine or glazing medium, or simply with a heated palette knife.

This recipe (Pratt, p. 35) is a variation on cold wax paste discussed in **Cold Wax for Encaustic** chapter.

You will need:

- 1 part wax
- 3 parts damar varnish.

Step one: Mix the wax and varnish in a glass jar. Seal the jar with a tight lid and gently shake the contents to fully incorporate the ingredients. Fred wanted you to let the glaze stand for three weeks or longer before using. But almost as soon as I added the varnish, the mixture became a thick, translucent jelly. I used it after five days, again after twelve days and finally used my last bit after nearly twenty days. The only change I noticed was that the goo became even more translucent over time.

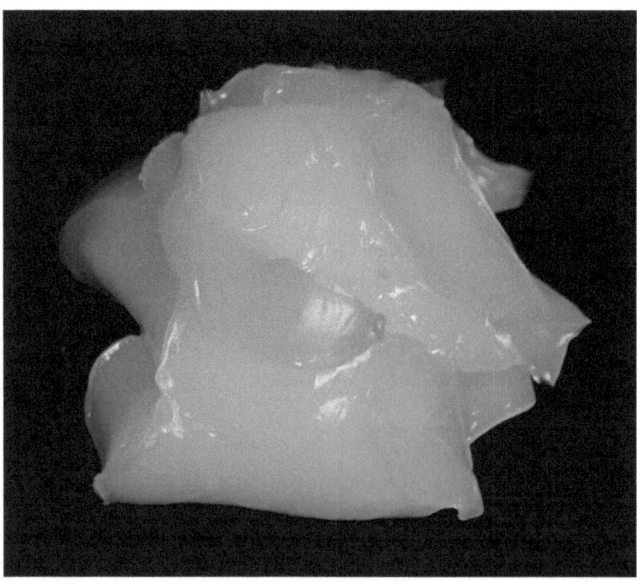

Two week-old cold wax paste made with damar varnish (damar crystals dissolved in turpentine). Use this as a basis for paint or by itself as a glaze.

Glazing: Pratt and Fizell noted that Conway used a brush or knife to apply the glaze to the painting surface. I actually globbed it on with a spoon and rubbed it off with a cloth, as you would furniture varnish. The piece will be dry in an hour or two, but you should wait 24-48 hours before fusing. The strong smell of turpentine will get less, and that's how you know the material has gassed off sufficiently for fusing. And use your heat gun. Your torch can catch it on fire. And yes, before you ask, I've done it.

Fred experimented with the proportions of wax to solvent. Using more wax, he developed a formula that could build heavy impasto surfaces. Using more turpentine, he made a thin glaze that could be sprayed onto the canvas with a simple pump sprayer.

The recipe above is lovely to handle. Add pigment to make a tinted glaze. By using a higher wax content you can develop a formula that is great for priming your encaustic panels, as discussed in the section on Cold Wax Saturated Boards. Cold wax made with damar varnish has good binding qualities that other solvents do not.

And don't forget that you can heat this substance on your palette or fuse gently with your heat gun.

Glaze comparison chart

After testing these glazes, I graded them on a six point scale, evaluating them according to such qualities as appearance, drying time, and bloom prevention. Here is my table of results:

	Half and Half	Aronson Glaze	Conway Glaze
Application method	Hot wax, brushed on.	Hot wax, applied with a knife.	Cold wax, brush or wipe on.
Drying time	Instant.	Up to two weeks.	24-48 hours.
Transparency	Cloudy, more than regular white wax medium.	Clear if applied thinly.	Clear if applied thinly.
Interaction with underlayers	None. I fused lightly to get a good bond.	None.	Slight interaction with top layer.
Appearance	Thick, semi-gloss.	Thin, gloss.	Medium body, eggshell finish
Bloom prevention	Very good.	Very good.	Very good

Paint Additives

Key paint ingredients and where to find them

I've mentioned several ingredients that you can add to hot or cold wax preparations. This chapter discusses where to buy these supplies and, in some cases, how to make them at home.

Damar Varnish

Damar varnish is nothing fancier than damar crystals dissolved in good quality turpentine. It is used as a classic picture varnish and as an additive to various paint recipes. Encaustic artists also use it to emulsify dry pigment. Although damar varnish is expensive to purchase in an art supply store, it's not difficult—or expensive—to make at home.

Homemade damar varnish

You will need:

- 1 quart glass or metal container with tight-fitting lid.
- Cheese cloth
- Fine string or dental floss
- 2 cups damar crystals
- 2 cups turpentine

Step one: Cut a square of cheesecloth two layers thick. Place the damar crystals in the center of the square and wrap the cloth around them, teabag style. Tie the bag closed with the dental floss, knotting it firmly. Leave an eight inch "tail" of dental floss.

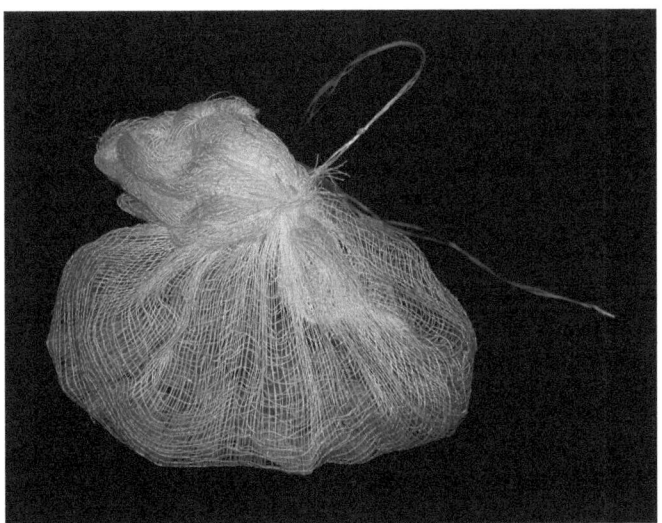

Bag-0-damar crystals, using cheesecloth and dental floss.

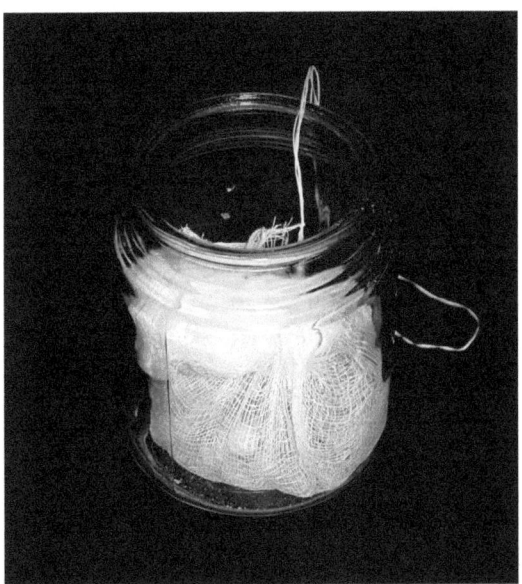

Damar bag placed in glass jar, tail left out.

Step two: Pour the turpentine into the 1-quart container. Place the bag of damar in the container, draping the string tail outside the container. Move the bag up and down in a dunking motion to wet the bag. Holding the end of the string so that the bag is suspended yet covered by turpentine catch the string between the lid and jar when you screw down the lid. The bag of resin should hang in the liquid. Place the jar on a high shelf away from pets and children.

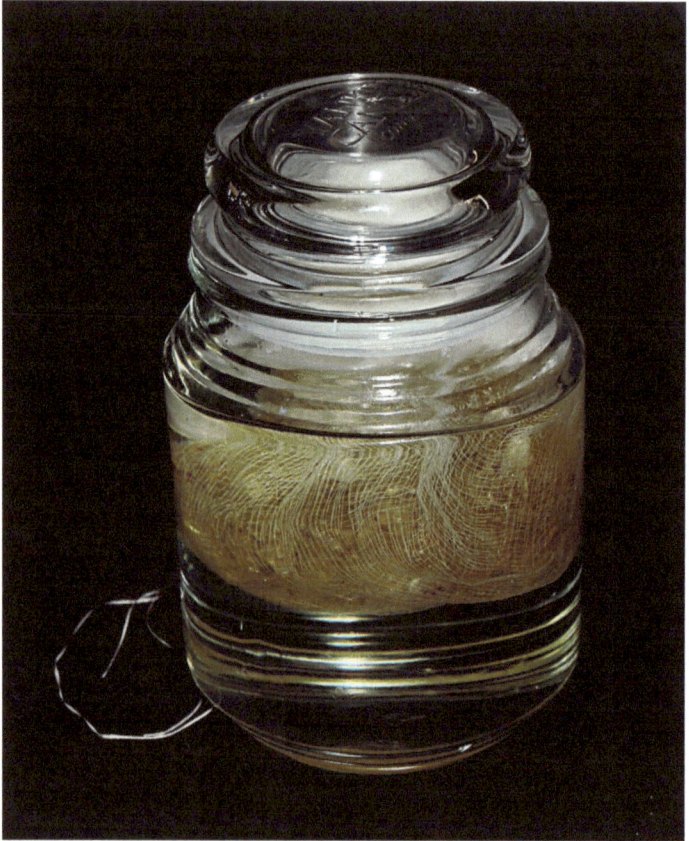

Turpentine and damar crystals, day one.

Generally, dental floss will not "wick" turpentine from the container. If you see turpentine dripping from the end of the string, drop it into the jar and reseal.

Step three: After a few days, check back. The damar should be fully dissolved, leaving nothing but splinters and pitch debris inside the cheesecloth bag. Remove the bag, placing it in a disposable plastic container. You can let it sit outdoors in a safe place until the turpentine evaporates before putting it in the garbage.

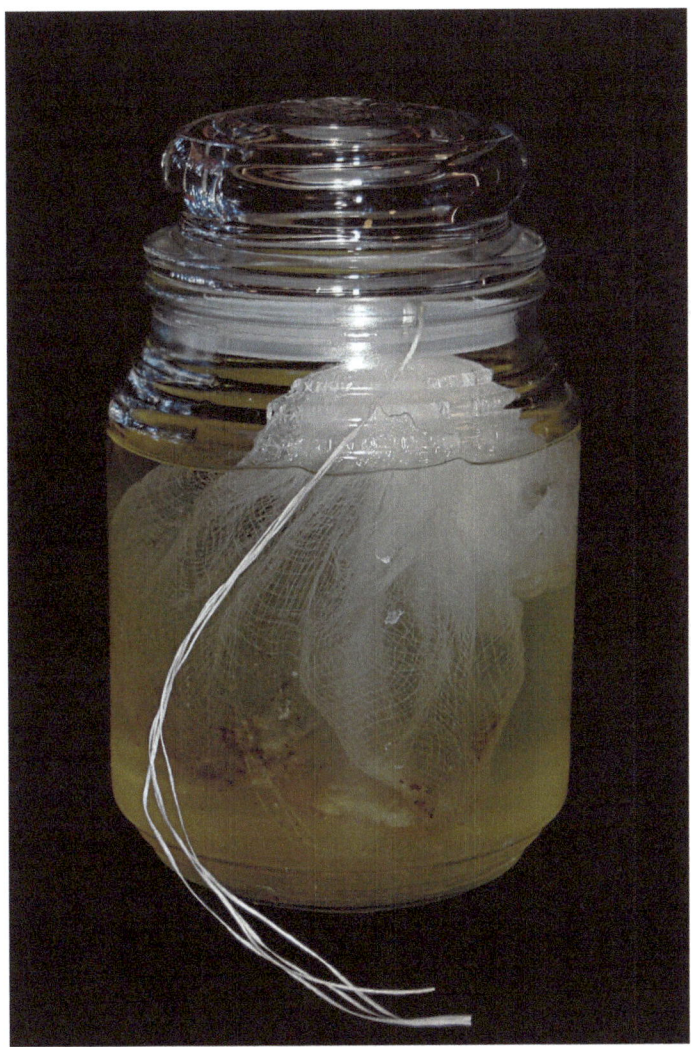

Finished damar varnish. After a week, all you can see in the bag are splinters.

The damar varnish should be thick and golden. Don't worry if it looks a little cloudy; there may be some waxy residue on the resin that dissolved along with the pitch. This is a slightly heavier concentration than the standard "5-pound cut." I use it as is, though it can be thinned and extended with more turpentine.

From here, you can use damar varnish to make cold wax medium or paint, or as an additive to hot wax paint.

Linseed Oil, Sun-Thickened Linseed Oil and Stand Oil

Linseed Oil

Linseed oil is made from crushed flax seeds and is most commonly used in oil painting as a drying oil. When exposed to the air, it forms a tough film rather like a skin on top of a cooling cup of coffee. It is used in encaustic paint as a vehicle for blending dry pigments. When added to dry pigment in a separate mixing tray, you can work the oil into the powder until it is smooth. Linseed oil will also help the pigment disperse into hot wax and keep the particles in suspension a little longer.

Adding linseed oil to your hot wax paint adds some flexibility to wax and lengthens the amount of time it takes to cool. I use it for intarsia or any technique where I want to scrape back layers but don't want to hurry. It's not unusual to wait several hours before paint made with linseed oil has fully hardened and the colors are clear. Although linseed oil is a tool that helps wax go on smoothly and can level uneven surfaces, each artist will have to find her own balance between drying time and paint quality.

Where to buy linseed oil:

You can buy "boiled" linseed oil by the quart at the hardware store. Boiled oil has been heated and partially thickened, but is not considered a fine art material. It has a dark yellow to light brown color, and may include some other drying ingredients. I don't mind the boiled version for most applications, and when I do care, I use stand oil. Cold-pressed linseed oil available at the art supply store is a much higher grade product.

Sun-Thickened Linseed Oil

I'm not sure if this works any better than linseed oil in its normal state, though Mark David Gottsegen, in *The Painter's Handbook,* (Gottsegen, pp. 75-76) says it is somewhat faster drying because it has already partially oxidized. You can make it at home, though where I live in Oregon's soggy Willamette Valley, it takes much longer than it would in, say, Tuscany.

Mix equal parts linseed oil and water in a clear glass container. Cover the mouth of the container with cheesecloth and place the container in a sunny window for several weeks. Mix occasionally. After several weeks, depending on the amount of sun, the mixture will develop a strip of pale, butter-like paste between the bottom layer of water and the surface layer of oil.

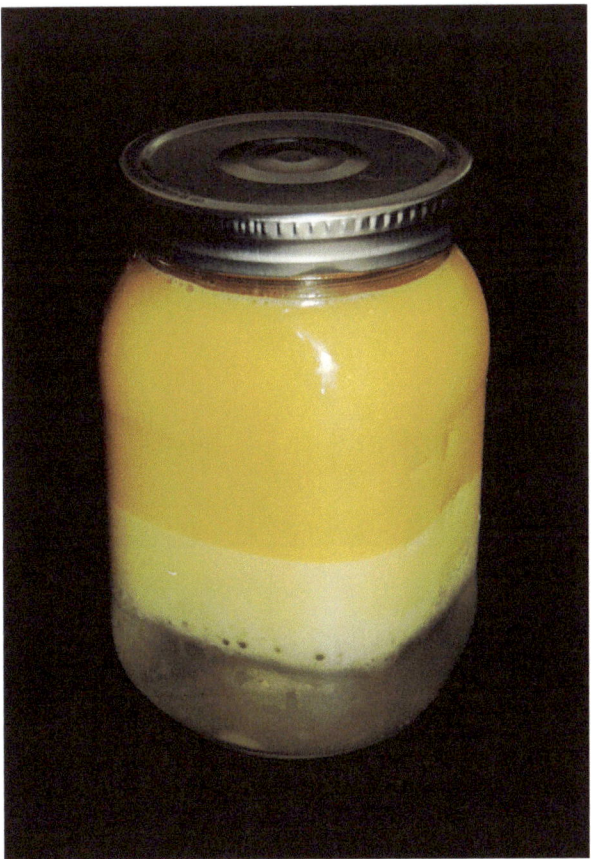

Here is a jar of linseed oil and water about a week into the process. The jar has a lid in place of the cheesecloth cover because I had just shaken the contents.

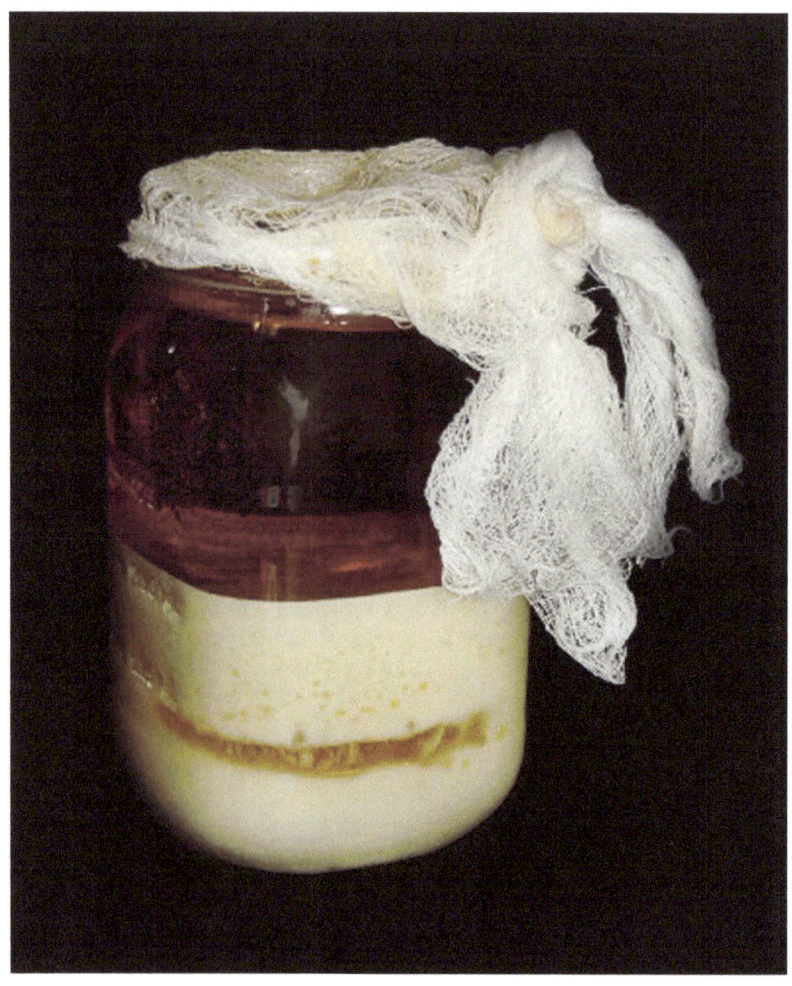

After three months, the soapy paste has separated from the thickened oil.

Keep mixing it once a week or so, using a whisk or paint stick or even by shaking it (with a lid on) to drive water and oil into the layer of paste. The process is done when the oil level above the white paste has thickened and turned a clear golden color. Transfer contents to a small jar by gently pouring the oil through a cheesecloth strainer.

Stand Oil

Stand oil is linseed oil that has been heated at a high temperature in a closed vessel for several hours, long enough for the substance to polymerize. Stand oil is a gloriously thick, honey-like substance and it is used in glaze and paint recipes for both traditional oil painting as well as encaustic. I've never seen any recipes for making it at home, but it's not that expensive at the art supply store, especially considering how little you will ever use at one time.

Turpentine and Mineral Spirits

Mineral Spirits

This is a petroleum-based product. Occasionally called paint thinner or white spirits, it is a solvent that can dissolve wax. When used in wax emulsion, it evaporates quickly, leaving only the waxy remains behind. It is considered slightly toxic and should be used in small quantities. Please dispose of unused portions according to the instructions on the container.

I use it to good effect as an encaustic board preparation. When applied repeatedly to a hot board, it can drive out gas bubbles leaving your encaustic painting free of pin holes. Read more about it in the chapter on **Cold Wax for Encaustic**.

Turpentine

Turpentine is refined and distilled pine pitch. It has a fairly low fire risk (compared to some of the other solvents) but prolonged exposure to turpentine vapors, or any direct contact with skin, should be considered hazardous. Odorless versions are available and are supposed to be good. I like the smell of turpentine; I heard another artist say once that walking into someone's studio and smelling turps and linseed oil fired the imagination to possibilities. All that aside, odorless turps is hazardous because you can't tell by smell whether you are inhaling too much. I buy the regular kind and expect my nose to tell me when I've left a container open on my worktable too long.

Ralph Mayer says that turpentine's rate of evaporation "…is exactly fitted to the great majority of paint and varnish purposes; that is, it allows sufficient time for brushing manipulations, and it evaporates rapidly enough for most users." (Mayer, p. 404)

What this means for encaustic is that if you choose to thin your wax paint with turpentine to achieve a wash-like effect, the turps will stay liquid and brushable for a little longer than plain wax. The more turpentine you add, the longer the paint takes to harden. The best form of turpentine to use for encaustic is **damar varnish**, which can be used in hot wax recipes as well as cold. If you are making a cold wax paint or glaze, use turpentine or damar varnish instead of mineral spirits.

Where to buy it:

If you are just starting out, buy your turpentine along with your linseed oil at any hardware, paint or building materials store. A quart typically costs $7 or $8.

Venice Turpentine

I have to admit I don't know much about Venice turpentine. It is a thick, resinous substance made from the pitch of the larch tree. Artists mix it with stand oil in glaze recipes because it is supposed to form a more flexible and non-yellowing film than other glazes. (Mayer, pp. 239-240) Here are two wax recipes featuring Venice turpentine, as reported by Frances Pratt and Becca Fizell in *Encaustic Materials and Methods*:

Karl Zerbe's wax-resin medium featuring Venice turpentine
(Pratt, p. 33)

You will need:

- 8 parts white beeswax
- 1 part damar resin crystals
- 1 part Venice turpentine

Melt the wax and add the damar crystals, heating until fully incorporated. Remove from heat, cool to 155-160 F and add the turpentine, a few drops at a time. This yields a hard, glossy medium that is good for wood panels and supports. This is a hot medium which can be cooled and reheated on your palette.

Fred Conway's Venice turpentine glaze (Pratt, p. 34)

You will need:

- 3 ½ parts beeswax
- 6 ½ parts Venice turpentine

Place wax and Venice turpentine in a glass jar, blend until the wax is soaked. Seal the jar with a tight-fitting lid and put aside for a week. If it is still lumpy after a week, wait another week. This glaze can be mixed with dry pigment or tube oil to make cold wax paint.

Where to buy Venice turpentine:

Sennelier offers a 32 milliliter tube which you can get at Utrecht for about $12.99. Check the web site first as not all brick-and-mortar stores will carry it. Commercially, Venice turpentine is used by farriers to treat horse hooves. Find it on Amazon, but be sure to check the other ingredients too.

Panels, Boards and Supports

Introduction to Supports

Here's something to consider about artists' materials: The art supply store is a fairly recent phenomenon. Think about Bisquick, everyone. Remember the yellow box with the fluffy pancakes on the label? Your mom probably had Bisquick in the pantry, and she may have had a couple of standard recipes she used time and again. They were printed right there on the box.

Bisquick is made of flour, salt, baking powder and shortening. Stuff your mom already had at home. What she was buying was the convenience and the recipes.

Art supply stores, with their pre-gessoed canvases and beautifully packaged paint sets, are like Bisquick because they shorten part of the preparation process and make it more predictable. And, sure, there are times when you want your results quick and predictable. But there are other times when you see something in your head—a color or texture or material—that won't exist until you invent it. Experimentation, trial and error, and practice are 98% of any artistic endeavor.

Almost any surface can function as a suitable support, even plexiglass and glass. Even if you are a beginner, you do not have to rely on standard sized or pre-made supports because almost any surface will do. However, encaustic suppliers make a full range of boards in all sizes, but an inexpensive packet of canvas practice boards work just as well – particularly if you are trying out new techniques or formulas. Some encaustic artists work on stretched canvas like an easel painter, though unsupported canvas is far too flexible for working with heavy impasto or multiple layers. Yet it can be done. In fact anything you can imagine, and a few things you can't, have been used as encaustic supports.

The same is true of your ground, which is the layer between the support and your first layer of wax. Some artists don't use a ground at all.

They prefer to lay their wax directly on the surface of a panel. The lessons of the ancient Greeks tell us that wood and wax are perfect partners, both organic and both aging into harder, drier forms of themselves.

Other artists prefer to have more control over their surface, sanding it and preparing it until it is a smooth, porous painting surface. Most prepared boards will come with a layer of white gesso on top, ready to use. A white under surface can create luminous paintings, which is sought after by many artists.

As we discuss how to make your own supports, keep in mind that there are few wrong answer in encaustic art - and why your own process of experiment and discovery is so important. You will learn what you like, and the images you see in your head will lead you to the materials and techniques you want to use.

Building Your Own Supports

Most prepared panels for encaustic painting come with some form of mounting hardware, but if you are making your own panels, you'll need some support structure. There are two reasons for doing this - one is practical, as it holds the panel rigid and flat; the other aesthetic, as it greatly influences how your finished work is displayed.

This is very easy, and requires no special tools or even any experience in woodworking. These instructions and suggestions are going to assume that you don't have any experience with woodworking - if you do, you already know everything I'm going to say, and don't need to read on.

We'll assume that you are using a rigid panel of some sort - either plywood or Masonite. The best, and also most economical, plywood for a painting surface is thin lauan plywood, also known as "underlayment." This hardwood plywood is typically about 1/4" thick, and is usually available in sizes from 2 x 4 feet up to full 4 x 8 foot sheets. Whether working on it directly, after preparing the surface, or covering it with paper or canvas you can still use these suggestions to cradle your panel.

There are basically two kinds of cradles: the recessed cradle and the full-size (edge) cradle. Assembly is essentially identical for both. You also have two ways to go about putting them together: DIY wood or pre-cut stretcher bars. The stretchers have the advantage of producing very professional looking results easily, though are rather more expensive, particularly if you work in larger sizes. You'll also be giving up some flexibility in terms of size and depth, but this is probably not an issue for most artists.

Materials and Tools

If you choose pre-cut stretcher bars, they typically come in full-inch common lengths (8, 10, 11, 12, 14, 16, 18, 20, 24 inches, and so on) and are typically about ¾' deep. For an 11 x 14 cradle, plan on spending $6.00-10.00. Larger sizes are, of course, more expensive – a 20 x 30 set will typically cost $10.00-20.00. The only other tools you will need are wood glue, wood filler and sandpaper.

Assembly of the pre-cut bars is very easy – the corners are what carpenters call a double-mortise, a kind of tongue-and-groove joint that slides together and is held with wood glue. Note that one side of the stretcher is curved, and the other flat. When used with canvas, the curved edge faces the painting surface for proper stretching. If you are using them with panels, though, you'll be better off mounting your panel to the flat side, again using wood glue – the flat surface provides a much better joint.

For the DIY approach, the first question is, of course, what kind of wood? As long as the lengths you need are fairly short (under about 24"), you can use "common" lumber, which may also be sold as "white wood" or "furring strips" – these are typically available in 1 x 2 and 1 x 3 sizes. This is very inexpensive - around here, you'd expect to pay about $1.25 for an 8 foot length of 1 x 2. Be careful, though, when selecting your wood - the pieces are often not perfectly straight (which is why they are less dependable in long lengths) and may have many imperfections (knots, torn edges, and so on). Expect that you may need discard quite a bit – but at about $.15 cents/foot, this is not your biggest worry. Also, remember that the actual dimensions of the wood are not quite what you might think – a 1 x 2 is actually closer to ¾ x 1 ½ and a 1 x 3 is approximately ¾ x 2 ½.

What tools are needed?

Nothing out of the ordinary. You'll need a saw of some sort, a hammer, finishing nails, wood glue and sandpaper. But what about that "saw of some sort"? Now the plot thickens. Your ideal is a saw that will let you make simple miter cuts (that is, angled) in light-grade wood – the 1 x 2 and 1 x 3. If you are beginning from absolute scratch on this, you should probably just buy a miter set (miter box and saw) – these are available at any good hardware or home improvement store for $10 to $50. The miter box is essentially a trough which holds your wood relative to pre-cut grooves. The miter saw moves in those grooves, and thus guarantees an accurate cut.

The Recessed Cradle

One of the best, and far the simplest, ways of mounting your panel, is the recessed cradle. In this, a rectangular frame smaller than your panel is attached to the rear side. It provides both structural stability - holding the panel flat - as well as making a very attractive way to hang your work without a frame.

Here's how to make one. Let's say your panel is 16 x 20 inches. Your cradle will be inset approximately 2-3 inches on each side, so let's say the finished dimensions of the cradle will be 10 x 14 inches. You'll need to decide how deep your cradle will be - for most smaller works, you'll probably do best with not more than about 1 ½ inches, though a larger work might look very striking with a deeper stand-off, say 2 ½ inches.

So, let's say you decide on the narrower (1 ½" cradle) - that means you'll be using 1 x 2 lumber. For our 10 x 14 inch cradle, you need 48 inches (10 + 14 + 10 + 14). Remember, though, if you are using the less expensive lumber, you'll need some extra wood so you can choose the best possible pieces.

There are two ways to make the joints for this cradle – carpenters call them a butt joint and a miter joint. With a butt joint, the two pieces of wood are both cut with "square" ends and joined end to end with glue and/or nails. With the miter joint, the frame pieces are cut at 45 degree angles and joined to make smooth corners. It's a bit trickier, but looks more professional. On the other hand, this form of cradle is invisible when the painting is hung, so a neatly done butt joint is also fine.

For either one, though, just measure your wood, slide it into your miter box, and make the cuts. Clean up the edges when you're done with a light sanding and glue or nail the pieces together. You can also easily do this, as should be obvious, with pre-cut stretcher bars.

Whichever method you use, when your cradle is assembled, attach it to the back of the panel using carpenter's wood glue. It can then also be easily hung from a pair of screws or, if you prefer, D-rings or a wire.

Simple, clean and inexpensive, yes. Perfect? Maybe – as long as you don't want your painting framed. If you know you will want your work framed, go on to the next section for the appropriate way to cradle your panel.

Purely personal choice here – some artists like to see their work "unframed" in this kind of floating mount, others feel a frame completes the effect of the work. You decide – it's your art.

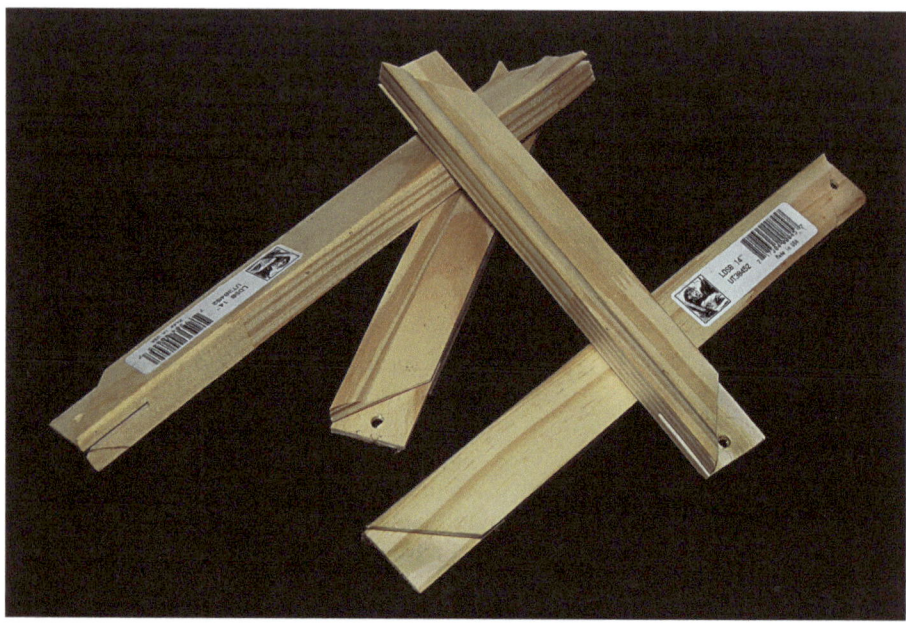

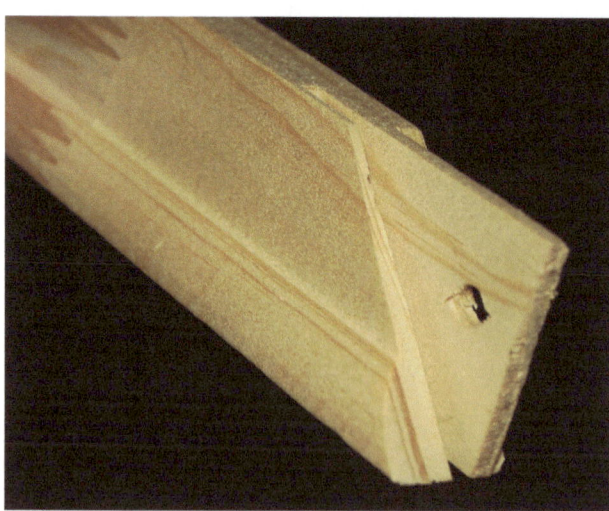

On top, a set of stretcher bars. Image below is a close-up of one end.

The Full-Size (edge) Cradle

If you would prefer to have the cradle extend to the edge of the panel, pre-cut stretcher bars become a more attractive option as the woodworking here requires some precision.

You can also, of course, do this by cutting your own pieces but since this cradle is far more visible (unless framed) in the finished work, the more complicated miter joints are very desirable. Remember – the simpler butt joint worked well for the recessed cradle, since the result was invisible when the painting was hung. So, unless you are fairly comfortable with woodworking, that is why you might want to go the pre-cut route here.

There is one additional step – since the edge of your panel is now flush with the cradle, you might want to finish that joint with wood filler. This is optional, though – try it both ways and see which you prefer. And it may be less important if you know the work is going to be framed.

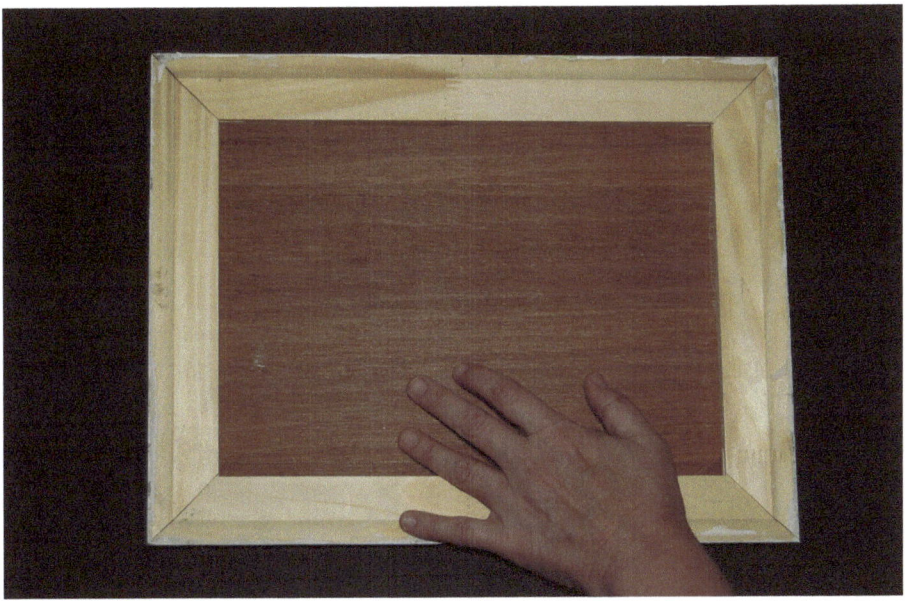

Back view of a cradled panel using stretcher bars.

A Note on Framing

Framing art work is the final step, but is almost always very expensive, if dealing with commercial framers (or even buying pre-made frames). It's also not something for the faint of heart to DIY, unless you have some fairly well-developed woodworking skills and tools.

With one exception. Yes, Virginia, there is a very easy and inexpensive way to frame your panels, and here is how.

Go to your local building supply store and buy some plain rectangular moulding – look for something about ¼" x 1 ½". You'll also need some fine gauge finishing nails and some sort of stain. For the latter, I'd recommend Minwax *Polyshade*, which is a hybrid stain/polyurethane that rubs on very easily.

But what you're doing with this could not be simpler. Start by fitting a piece to one side of the painting - it should extend just far enough beyond the edge of the canvas to meet the framing pieces on the adjoining sides. A miter box is helpful here but, frankly, the wood is so thin that (particularly if the finish color is dark), the seams are hardly perceptible. Cut two more pieces for the adjoining sides. Finally cut a piece to fit the remaining side. While you are working they can be held in position by finishing nails tapped halfway through the moulding into the stretcher - only partially sunk, though, for easy removal.

With the four pieces cut, remove them from the painting, clean up the ends and edges with a light sanding, and apply your finish. When dry, remount them with more finishing nails, this time tapped fully in. If the stretcher is not very deep, say c. ¾" to 1", do the final installation with the painting face down but held up with some spacers (strips of foamcore or a few layers of corrugated cardboard work very well) to give a bit of relief on the front edge of the frame.

This type of frame, particularly if you use the much simpler butt joint (rather than the miter joint) is going to have a much looser, informal look. It's a great way to keep pieces around the house or studio without spending a fortune. You might want something a bit more sophisticated for a gallery presentation – but maybe not. Try this out, work carefully, and I think you'll like the results. Also, it's a great way to protect the surface of your paintings – that small front lip can help keep panels from rubbing together in storage.

Encaustic Tools

Heating and hand tools for your studio

Ever wonder why handymen have so many different screwdrivers and wrenches in the toolbox? It's because each one has a slightly different purpose. And you always need a backup of course. What if you lose one?

Now multiply that by ten. You are an artist and the search for tools has become your newest obsession. You'll go through kitchen drawers looking for cookie cutters and frosting spreaders; you'll visit the art supply store and stand in the clay aisle hefting wire tools; you now care a lot about natural bristle vs. artificial bristle brushes.

Go to an artist's studio and check out their tools. They will have many high-end torches and hake brushes, tacking irons and heat guns. But they will also have a handful of the grubbiest, weirdest looking things, all caked with wax. These are the tools that feel good in the hand, which the artist has discovered and put to use. I have a rat-tail file and an old folding pocket knife. These tools always work and there isn't much that can go wrong with them.

So where do you begin your quest for the perfect encaustic tools? Let's start with the big stuff:

Heating tools

Heated palette

This is the heart and soul of the operation. This is where you melt medium, mix colors, and clean your brushes. A heated palette can be as simple as an electric griddle, electric frying pan or hotplate. It must have a wide, flat surface, a thermostat and a temperature gauge. You can buy heated palettes designed for encaustics, but they aren't any more sophisticated—or reliable—than your basic electric griddle. Plus they cost a small fortune.

Old griddles frequently turn up at garage sales (along with Crock-Pots) and I usually pay no more than $5 for an electric griddle. That way I'm not heart-broken if my current palette breaks down, and I can afford to keep a couple of spares on the shelf. That said, some of those old kitchen griddles seem to last forever.

Another nice quality of electric griddles is that they often have gutters running around the edges. This was probably to catch extra fat when mom was frying bacon, but works well for those of us who spill wax on the palette surface. Not me! I never accidentally dump tins of medium on my palette and have to scrape it off the table and, um, floor.

Since temperature accuracy isn't always a sure thing with heated palettes, no matter where they came from, you might want a handy little surface thermometer. Wish I had one!

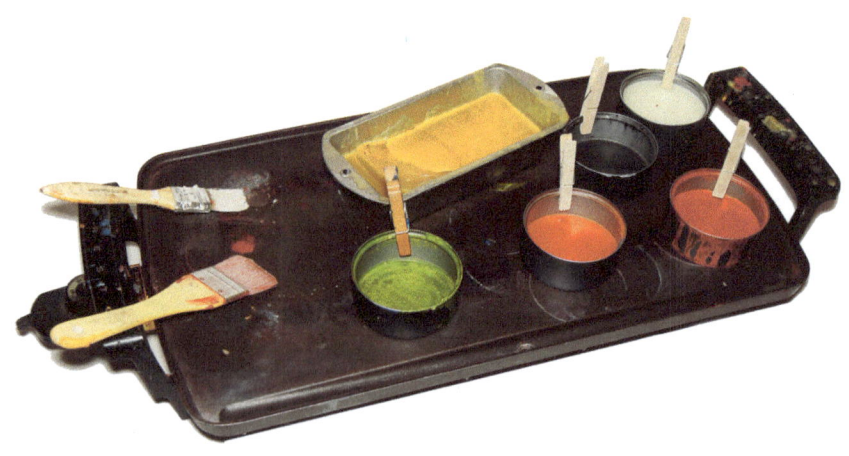

This palette, another yard sale find, has been going strong for four years. Pretty good for $5!

Crock-Pots

I think Crock-pots are a great idea for keeping a large amount of wax medium warm, melted and ready for use. However, I do not encourage the use of slow cookers for making batches of wax medium. They are very large and heavy and most aren't designed for pouring. Another issue to consider is how much electricity they require. Is it worth it? Read the **Studio Safety** chapter for more information about electricity in the studio.

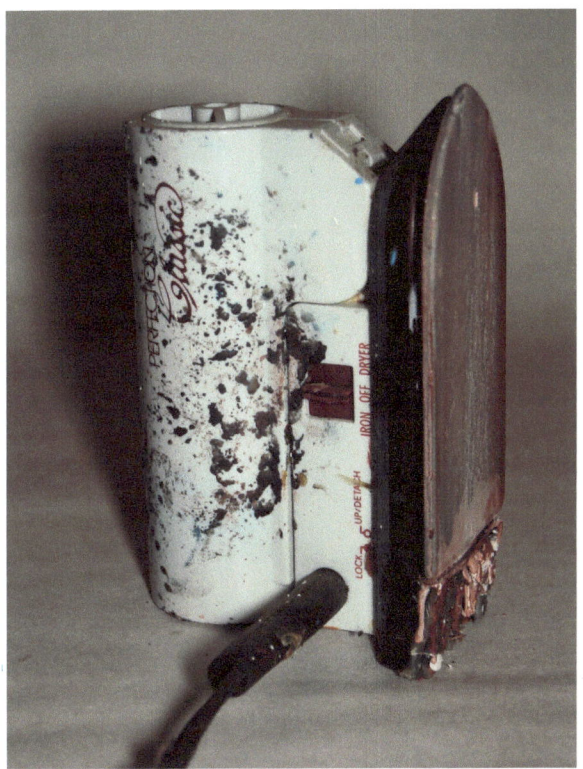

My travel iron has logged more miles on encaustic than it ever did in the air.

Electric Iron

My first fusing tool was an iron. Irons apply heat to the wax by direct contact, which is different than any other heating tool. With it you can create a perfectly smooth, "ironed" surface. Irons also blend colors. If you ever want to make your own Mark Rothko painting in encaustic, you'll use an iron. If you look closely at the encaustic paintings of Jasper Johns, you will sometimes find the imprint of an iron. By now the leaf shape and vent holes of this humble household tool has become iconic.

While using direct heat like an iron, I learned to hate acrylic additives in paint. There's nothing like pulling the iron off a painting and seeing cheese strings of melted plastic stuck to the iron. If you use an iron, make extra certain your prepared surface doesn't have acrylic paint or polymer binders in it.

I use a small travel iron with no steam vents on the bottom. It only has two settings: **on** and **off**. I've had encaustic irons too, but generally found them frustrating. You want an iron where the cord doesn't detach from the body of the tool whenever you flick your wrist. There are times when added safety features, such as an on-board plugin, make the tool unsafe. Plugging it back in all the time increases your chances of burning yourself.

Heat gun

Heat guns are basically super-charged hairdryers. They move a lot of very hot air, and for this reason you should think of them as diffuse heating tools. I use mine to pre-heat prepared surfaces, for fusing base layers, and for fusing color fields.

Heat guns come in various strengths and wattages. Mine is a solid, mid-line tool you can find at any hardware or paint store. There is no advantage to getting the hottest or strongest heat gun because you aren't melting anything much above 200° F. As a general rule, hold the gun 12" to 14" away from your painting to start and keep the nozzle moving across the painting in even strokes. If you linger too long in one place, you'll get a bare spot. Stop heating when the wax begins to glisten. Any longer and you'll be surprised how quickly the wax "pops" into liquid and flows everywhere, driven by the forced air.

Possibly the single greatest use of a heat gun is melting your tins of wax medium and paints in a hurry. Some days that's all I use it for.

Note: The heat gun is also the best tool for fusing cold wax—a torch is not safe for use with solvents. Use your heat gun.

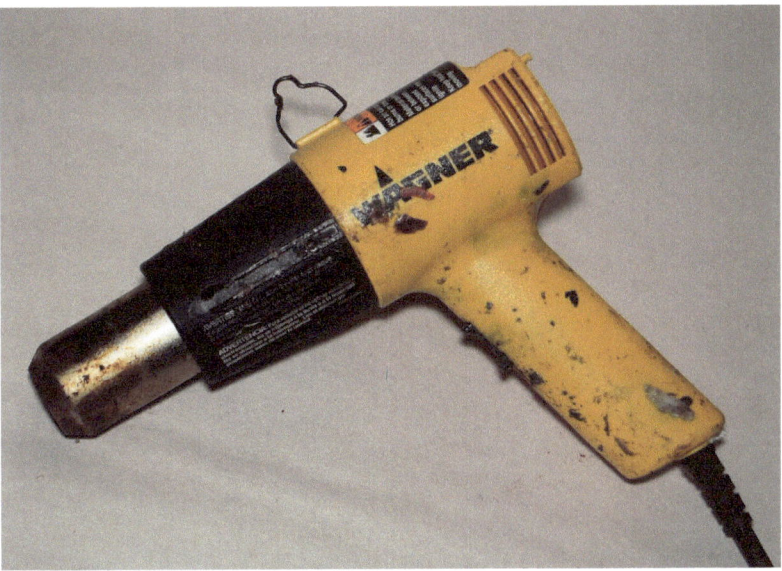

Heat gun, an encaustic artist's best friend...

Torch

Handheld butane or propane torches come in all sizes and shapes, and every artist has a favorite. Because these are a significant investment, try out several kinds before committing yourself. I have small hands so I use a professional-quality crème brulee torch with push-button ignition and an on-board fuel gauge.

Some artists use torch heads attached to cans of fuel. These are great tools, very effective for diffuse heating, but again, heft the weight of one of these units and fit your hand around a can of fuel before buying. You're going to spend a lot of time with this tool; it might as well be comfortable.

A torch doesn't force as much air as a heat gun, and you can focus the tip of the flame as widely or narrowly as you want. You don't overheat as much, or heat areas that don't need it. With a torch you can work very close to the painting, fusing precisely.

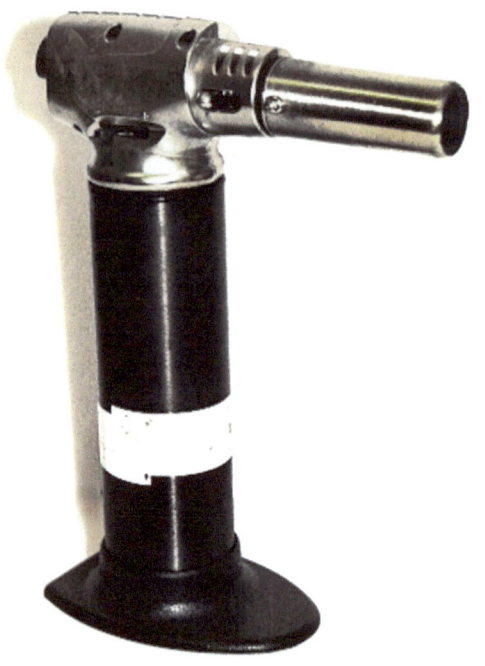

The perfect torch for whipping up creme brulee,
lighting the barbecue and laying down a few coats
of encaustic wax.

Here's another tiny torch. Sadly, it has to be relit each time you use it. It's great for small wax repairs, like when my cat left five deep gouges in a favorite encaustic piece. No, I didn't use it on him! I wanted to but The Theory said no.

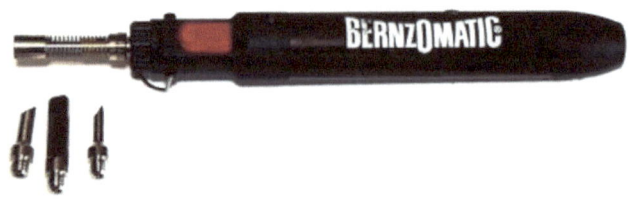

Tins and Pots

I have hundreds of cat food tins, 20 assorted other tins, a stack of muffin tins, a bunch of loaf pans, four large melting pots, and guess what? That's not enough. And jars? Let me tell you—jam jars, caper jars, pickle jars. I've got dozens. *I want more.*

When I started making wax medium, I used cat food tins. These are still perfect vehicles for wax, and I have an endless supply, thanks to all the feline freeloaders on the payroll. The best tins are solid metal, not coated with plastic. 9 Lives makes a good cat food tin for encaustic medium. Unfortunately, it's not the favorite food of the herd, so I sneak in a few weeks of 9 Lives meals per year whether they like it or not.

Of course you can buy tins designed for encaustic paint, but why bother? Here's another time that garage sales and Goodwill are really what you want. No one keeps their fancy, Teflon-coated muffin tins. They all end up on the shelf at Goodwill where you can pick them up for $2.99. And little metal bowls? Why were they made if not for encaustic paint? Pick them up whenever you see them.

Pots and pans for melting wax are at Goodwill too. You can't use the ones in your kitchen (okay, you *can* but how are you going to cook dinner?), so buy a good used set. Buy extras. When you are making art, you want to have the right tools for the job at hand. Make sure the handles are sturdy and well attached. Also, make sure you can lift the pan when it's full.

And my last word of advice about tins and pans—get more than you think you'll need because you're going to need a lot.

Hand Tools

Although there are a variety of encaustic tools available, wait to buy them. Instead, go directly to the printmaking and pottery aisles of your nearest art supply store and buy these tools:

- **--Lino Cutter** and a package of extra blades (printmaking, about $7.00)
  The blades channel cut, removing strips of wax rather than furrowing wax along the sides like a snowplow. You can also heat

the blades on your palette for an extra smooth cut. This tool is worth every penny!

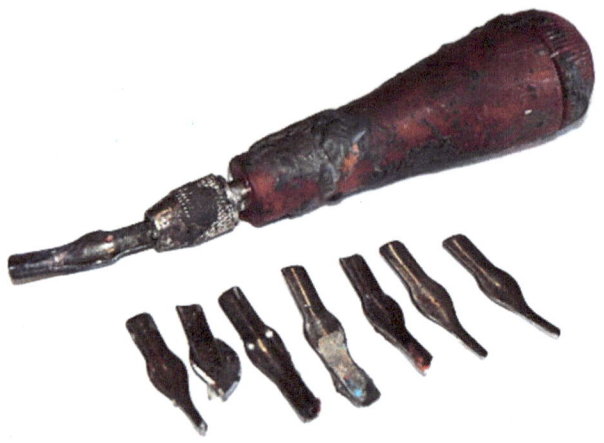

From the grubbiness of this tool, you can tell I use it a lot.

- **Mini-ribbon tools** (pottery, about $8). You'll find these in the pottery aisle. These are small tools with a metal handle and thin little wire loops on top, and you'll usually find them in packaged sets with different tips. These tools are far sturdier than regular ribbon tools. Use them for scraping excess wax from inlayed wax lines. Sadly, these guys don't last long. The wires bend out of shape or break after a few weeks. Buy an extra package.

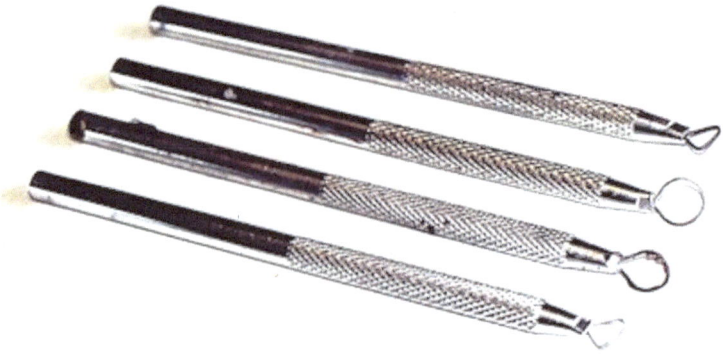

Small but mighty, those little metal ribbons make cleaning up your incised lines so incredibly easy.

- **Wooden pottery tools** (pottery, $2 each). There is a whole range of solid wooden tools for clay that work well with wax. Burnishing tools and scraping tools abound. They are cheap and feel good in the hand. Don't buy the plastic ones. Plastic tools will not hold up to heat.

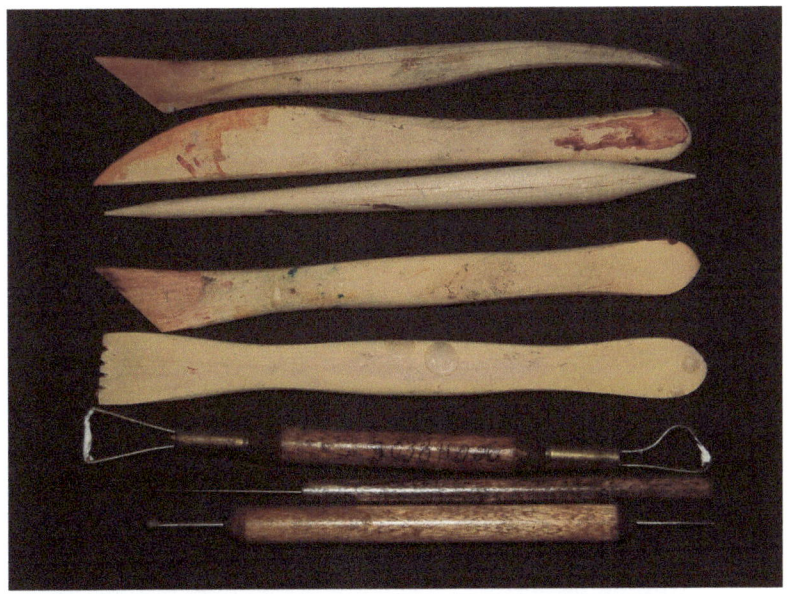

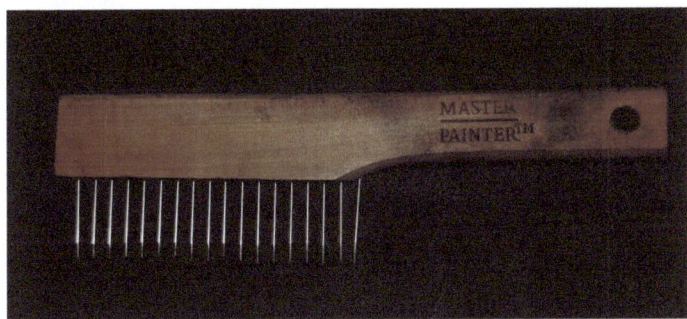

Wooden hand tools. The top image shows clay tools, the lower image shows a steel comb I found in a hardware store paint department. It's very sturdy, almost unbreakable. Or at least I haven't broken it yet.

- **Stainless steel sculpting tool set** (sculpture, $12). This set of small steel tools and picks with different-shaped heads is extremely tough and rigid. I didn't buy these tools until I'd been doing encaustic for several years, but I now use them constantly for incising small lines, scraping and scumbling.

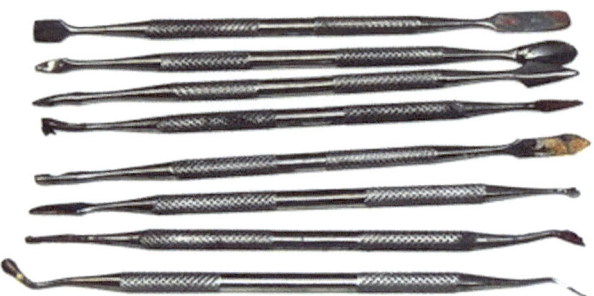

Stainless steel sculpting tools that would probably work great as dental instruments.

Brushes

Encaustic artists prefer the flat, rugged Hake brush. It is a wash brush, intended to add water or washes to large painting areas. They are tough enough for hot wax and come in a variety of sizes from 5/8" to 3." Buy only natural bristle brushes, and start with two or three in the 1" to 2" range and a 3" brush for applying medium and gesso. In the store, give the bristles a tug to make sure none are loose and likely to come out in your paint. You will probably buy more brushes every time you go to the art store from now on.

- **Studio brushes**. These are definitely more expensive, and you will guard them with your life, but a couple of bright or flat studio brushes with natural bristles are just about the sweetest treat you can give yourself.

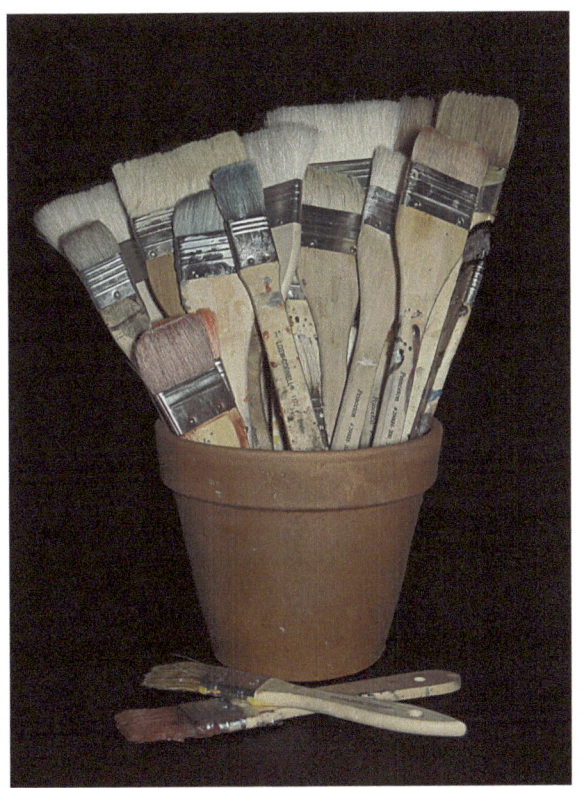

Never enough brushes, especially since cheap hake brushes (my favorites) tend to expire right in the middle of projects. Great re-purposing of a flower pot.

Caring for brushes

Encaustic is pretty cool this way. If you leave your brush sitting in a can of wax paint and the wax hardens, all you have to do is melt the paint. Your brush is fine. Some people keep a set of brushes for each color, but when I try to do that I never have the brush I need when I need it. Now I try to clean my brushes between uses, even though I understand I'll never get all the color out of the bristles. Here are a couple of cleaning ideas:

- **Melted soy wax.** I didn't believe it at first but soy wax works as a brush cleaner. Dip the brush in melted soy wax and wipe it down with a clean rag. Heat the brush on the palette to melt more wax and repeat.

- **Mineral spirits or turpentine.** Okay, this may not be good encaustic practice but I usually keep some mineral spirits around to clean brushes. Pour a small amount in a can, dip the brush in and swirl it around. Wipe it down with a clean rag. Done.

Miscellaneous Tools

- **Clothes pins.** Buy at any craft store, $1.99 to $2.99 per package. Get wooden pins with the wire spring. Attach a clothes pin to a hot can of wax and you have an instant handle for scooting the can around your palette.
- **Cotton rags.** You will need more cotton rags than you think. Cut up your old sheets and keep an eye out at garage sales. You can also buy bags of rags at a hardware store, though they tend to shed more than old household linens.
- **Craft sticks**. Buy these at any craft store, $1.99 to $4.99 per packet. These are great for mixing and labeling colors. You can even use them to dip wax onto your painting.
- **Cotton swabs**. I use these for mixing linseed oil with pigment. Dispose of immediately, the cotton threads will come off in your paint.
- **Metal mixing tray or mini-muffin tin**. Buy them at any craft or art supply store. In fact, buy two. Each tray has six or eight mixing wells. It's incredibly convenient to mix colors in the wells and pour into your heated wax.
- **Microfiber hand towels**. You can usually find packages of these at your local dollar store. These are soft, reusable towels that are ideal for buffing your finished paintings. You can also use other soft fabrics for polishing, but these microfiber cloths work great.
- **Paper towels**. Use these for cleaning out mixing trays and tins of wax.
- **Pliers and vise grips**. These are the tools you need for gripping, lifting and pouring those extremely hot tins full of melted wax. Keep a couple of pairs around—I am always losing them.

Toxicity of Art Materials

Those deadly poisons that make beautiful colors

If I haven't already said this, I'll say it again: an artist's studio can be the home equivalent of a superfund site. There are untold numbers of toxic chemicals that can infiltrate your body as particulate matter (such as pigments, plaster dust, sawdust or anything that floats in the air), as vapors (turpentine and other volatile solvents), or absorbed through the skin (tube oils, dry pigments).

Even now artists die from long-term exposure to their art materials. For every item in your studio, there's at least one artist who died from it—and usually many more. Take pigment, for instance. Flake white is a lead-based pigment, and lead poisoning is a legendary killer of humans and wildlife.

Dry pigments are toxic and dangerous in any form. Read Ralph Mayer's extensive chapter on pigments (Mayer, pp. 29-166) and just admit, as I have, that it makes no sense to try to remember which pigments are deadly carcinogens and which are just irritating. Treat them all as if they are nuclear waste. Modern pigments can be made from cobalt, strontium, cadmium, and arsenic, among others. You do not want these compounds to touch you. Since these are often the brightest and prettiest colors, they are probably safer if purchased as oil paints where the oil content renders them nearly harmless, unless you eat the paint or smear your body with it. Don't.

For basic safety, use a face mask respirator, latex gloves, and cover any exposed skin. Safest of all is to use a "chemical glove box" for handling pigments. Search the internet for cheap and easy DIY glove boxes, which can be made with a clear, lidded storage bin, latex gloves, plastic "sleeves" and duct tape.

As bad as pigments are, volatile solvents are considered the most toxic. All solvents are toxic, even something as common as turpentine. However, most materials can be safely handled if you read the instructions on the jar or can, and dispose of leftovers appropriately. If you are trying a new substance, read up on it first. Find out what it does and how to handle it.

Always keep on hand the following basic safety tools:

- Disposable gloves
- Face masks—ideally, we'd all use respirators
- Safety glasses

These items can be purchased at your local hardware store inexpensively. And it's no good having them on your work table collecting dust—**you have to put them on for them to work**.

Studio Safety

Infrastructure support for your studio

After all the art supplies, paint, fillers, binders and media, your ability to function as an artist depends on three important considerations: Security, electricity and ventilation. Oh, and one more: Fire hazard.

Security: Lock your door

Art studios are full of interesting aromas, touchable objects and pretty colors. Your children, pets, friends and nosy relatives may not be aware of the hazards, so it is always a good idea to have a lock on your studio door.

Electricity: A special consideration for encaustic studios

Have I mentioned electricity? To me, electricity used to be an invisible force that came out of plugs in the walls and made things work. I always seemed to have enough. And then one day I fired up my electric palette, iron and heat gun and blew every fuse in the studio. The problem was this: My studio had 15 amps of power. Just running the overhead lights and a heater, I was using almost half of that.

Amps, volts, watts

The Theory provided me with this handy equation:

1 amp x line voltage (most common being 110 volts) = 110 watts

My studio ran 15 amps which gave me about 1600 watts. That sounded like a lot of juice until I realized my heat gun pulled 1200 watts every time

I turned it on, my palette required about the same all the time, and I still needed lights and a space heater.

An electrician came in and re-wired the studio, putting it on its own circuit. Now I have 75 amps of power and I can even listen to music while I work.

Most modern homes have about 100 amps, which is sufficient for anything a family needs. But if you are concerned, ask an electrician to take a look. Not having enough electricity will make you feel like an ancient Greek very quickly.

Fire Hazard: Hot to the touch

Never forget you are using a viscous liquid heated to nearly 200 degrees Fahrenheit. Heated much beyond that, wax will burn. So will everything else.

- You need a fully charged **fire extinguisher** close to hand. No exceptions. Even if you never use your extinguisher, you should have your unit checked and topped off every year.
- Keep a pail of water in your studio for burns. I have a watering can, same thing.

Less obvious but equally important is the layout of your studio and work tables.

- Use large, sturdy work surfaces.
- Avoid excess clutter whenever possible, especially around hot tools.
- Give yourself plenty of room to move around.
- Keep all electrical cords out of the way. Cords are *always* a tripping hazard.
- Concrete floors are best, but if you don't have them, lay down smooth, rigid, flame-resistant flooring.

Ventilation

I'm rarely bothered by the smell of paint and turpentine. With artists for parents, I grew up in art studios and those are deceptively comforting smells for me. They say you can get used to anything, right? This early conditioning means that I have to be extra careful about ventilation because these smells don't *seem* harmful to me.

The fact is, all artists need fresh air to diffuse the toxicity of their materials. Even beeswax can release irritants as it heats up. Probably the best way to solve this problem is to work in a big space, not a crowded closet. Make sure you have two windows that can open, one on either side of the room, and keep them open. Take frequent breaks. It helps to have a couple of large dogs who want in and out all the time—what you won't do for yourself you'll do for a pet.

Note: For those of us with small studios (such as a windowless closet), consider talking to an expert in ventilation to determine the best way to keep your air clean and moving.

Appendix A: Wax Melting Point Chart

Temperatures are given in Fahrenheit:

Coconut	110°F
Soy, bayberry	113°F
Paraffin, check packaging for range	120, 130, 140, 150°F
Beeswax	144-147°F
Candelilla	155-162°F
Impasto modeling wax	170°F
Microcrystalline, multiwax	175-200°F
Carnauba	179-186°F
Montan	179-200°F

Appendix B: Weights and Measures

Handy list of weights and measures based on the universal measuring unit at the Hive Encaustic--cat food tins:

- 1 cat food tin = ½ cup liquid wax
- 1 pound of melted wax medium = 4 cat food tins (not filled to top)
- 2.5 ounces of damar crystals = ½ cup crystals crushed to roughly the size of pinto beans
- 1 pound of wax prill = 3.2 cups dry measure
- 5 pounds of wax prill = 16 cups dry measure

Appendix C: How to Apply Gesso

Both traditional gesso and encaustic gesso are appropriate for wood panels.

You will need:

- Clean, dry board or canvas-mounted board
- Gesso, mixed according to the package directions and kept warm on your palette
- Clean, wide brush, like a housepainter's brush
- Package of fine sandpaper, grit sizes 180 to 400

Step one: Brush the warm gesso onto the surface of the support in clean, even strokes, going in one direction only. Allow the panel to dry. In Oregon drying can take from three hours to over night.

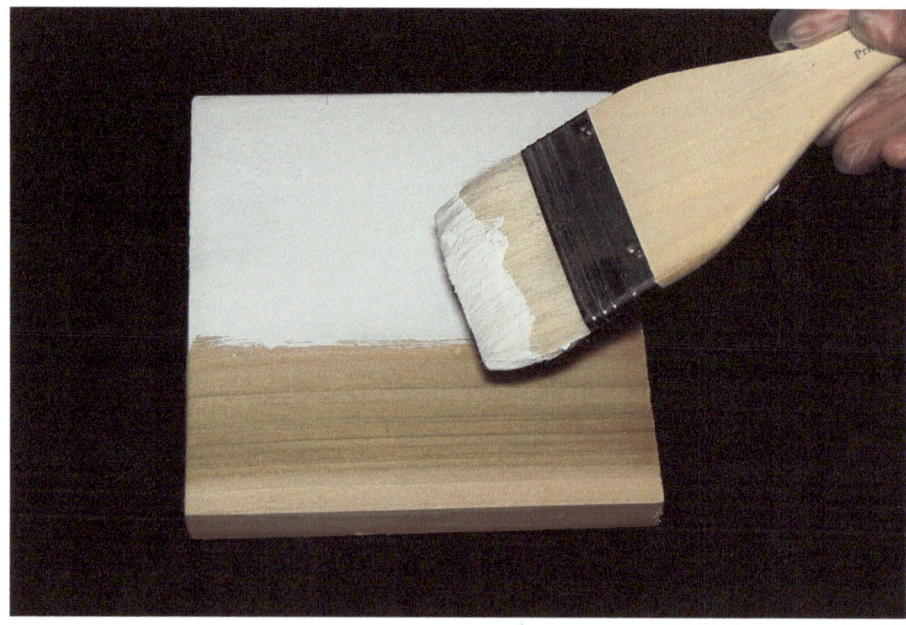

I'm applying traditional gesso ground.

Step two: Wrap a piece of sandpaper around a flat block of wood and sand the dry surface, using circular motions. When you get a smooth, even surface you can add another layer of gesso and repeat, or stop here. There's no rule about how many layers of gesso to add for encaustic work.

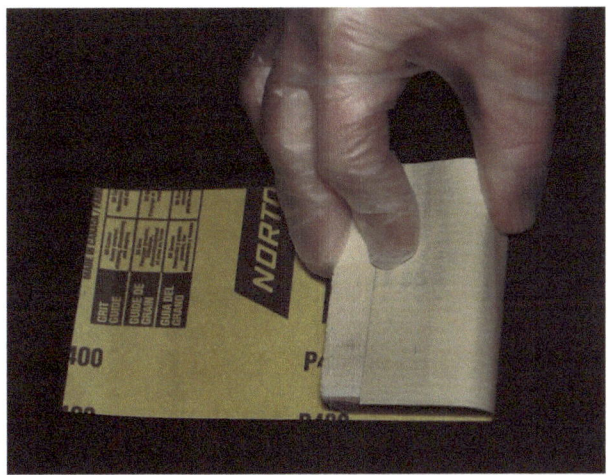

I cut the sandpaper to fit a small block.

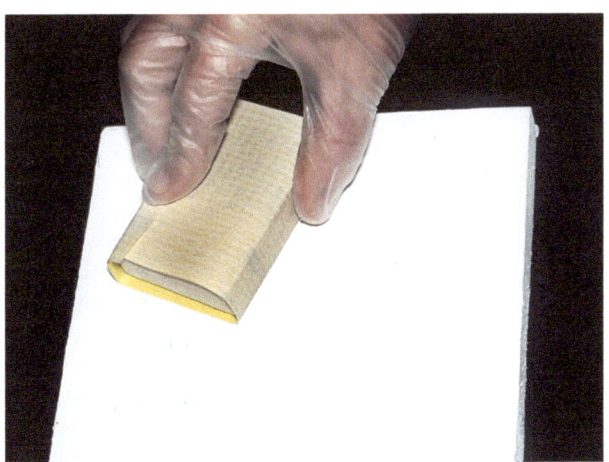

Start sanding with a course grit of sandpaper, but go gently as gesso is very soft. Aim to smooth large ripples, sanding left to right, turning the board 90 degrees and continuing. Work your way up to a fine grit, something like 400. But don't overdo it.

Step three: If you choose to add another layer, turn the board 90 degrees to your right and apply another coat of gesso. Use the same even, one direction strokes as before, but because you've turned the board your strokes won't magnify the stroke patterns of the first application. This is a really good habit to get into for applying wax medium as well. Allow the panel to dry and sand as before.

Note: Gesso can warp unbraced wood. A cradled panel (see instruction in the **Panels, Boards and Supports** chapter) will rarely warp. If you are using a single piece of unbraced wood, paint the reverse side with a quick coat of gesso to counter warping.

Appendix D: Encaustic Supplies

Dick Blick Art Materials—Cheap source for small tools and brushes of all kinds. Online catalog of dry pigments is a good resource.
http://www.dickblick.com/

Earth Pigments—Not just beautiful pigments. Great source for chalk, lime and other painting supplies, and a detailed recipe resource.
http://www.earthpigments.com/

Enkaustikos—Purveyors of Hot Cakes wax paint.
http://www.encausticpaints.com/

Evans Encaustics—Makers of Holy Grail encaustic gesso.
http://www.evansencaustics.com/

Miles Conrad—Distinctive wax paint colors.
http://www.custom-encaustics.com/

Milk paint—two milk paint sources:
The Old Fashioned Milk Paint Company http://www.milkpaint.com/
The Real Milk Paint Company http://www.realmilkpaint.com/

Natural Pigments—Beautiful colors and materials, source for Rublev pigments, some of which are available in bulk.
http://www.naturalpigments.com/

R&F Handmade Paints—Biggest and best, and not just a paint store.
http://www.rfpaints.com/

Ruhl Bee Supply—Filtered yellow beeswax from Ruhl is the sweetest.
http://www.ruhlbeesupply.com/

Swan's Candles—Bulk wax at reasonable rates, good shipping options.
http://www.swanscandles.com/

Utrecht Art Supplies—Good source for bulk damar crystals.
http://www.utrechtart.com/

Appendix E: Art and Encaustic Books

Gottsegen, Mark David. *The Painter's Handbook: A Complete Reference, Revised and Expanded* (New York: Watson-Guptill Publications, 2006).

Mattera, Joanne. *The Art of Encaustic Painting* (New York: Watson-Guptill Publications, 2001).

Mayer, Ralph. *The Artist's Handbook of Materials and Techniques, 5th ed.* (New York: Viking Penguin, 1991).

Pratt, Frances and Becca Fizell. *Encaustic Materials and Methods* (New York: Lear Publishers, Inc. 1949). Out of print, but visit http://francesprattart.com/ for updates about the forthcoming re-release.

Rankin, Lissa. Encaustic Art: The Complete Guide to Creating Fine Art with Wax (New York: Watson-Guptill Publications, 2010).

Roberts, Paul. *Mummy Portraits from Roman Egypt* (London: The British Museum Press, 2008).

Seggebruch, Patricia Baldwin. *Encaustic Workshop: Artistic Techniques for Working with Wax* (Cincinnati, Ohio: North Light Books, 2009).

Seggebruch, Patricia Baldwin. Encaustic Mixed Media: Innovative Techniques and Surfaces for Working with Wax (Cincinnati, Ohio: North Light Books, 2011).

Stavitsky, Gail. *Waxing Poetic: Encaustic Art in America* (Montclair, New Jersey: The Montclair Art Museum, 1997).

Taylor, William Benjamin Sarsfield. *A Manual of Fresco and Encaustic Painting* (London: Chapman Hall, 1843).

Womack, Bill and Linda. *Embracing Encaustic: Learning to Paint with Beeswax* (Portland, Oregon: Hive Publishing, 2008).

Woolf, Daniella. *Encaustic with a Textile Sensibility* (Waxy Buildup Press, 2010).

Woolf, Daniella. *The Encaustic Studio: a Wax Workshop in Mixed Media Art.* (Loveland, Colorado: Interweave, Inc., 2012).

Works Cited

A.J.'s Arts and Designs. (n.d.). Retrieved May 2013, from
http://www.ajsartsanddesigns.com/2011/01/my-homemade-gesso-recipe.html

Gottsegen, M. D. (2006). *The Painter's Handbook: A Complete Reference, Revised and Expanded.* New York: Watson-Guptill Publications.

Mattera, J. (2010). *The Art of Encaustic Painting.* New York: Watson-Guptill Publications.

Mayer, R. (1991). *The Artist's Handbook of Materials and Techniques, 5th edition.* New York: Viking Penguin.

Milk-Lime Paint. Retrieved May 2013, from Earth Pigments:
http://www.earthpigments.com/casein/milk-lime-paint.cfm

Pistrucci Artworks. (n.d.). Retrieved May 2013, from
http://pistrucciartworks.wordpress.com/2012/10/12/figure-drawing-chalkboard-paint/

Plaster of Paris. Retrieved May 2013, from Wikipedia:
http://en.wikipedia.org/wiki/Plaster_of_Paris#Gypsum_plaster_.28plaster_of_Paris.29

Pratt, F. a. (1949). *Encaustic Materials and Methods.* New York: Lear Publishers, Inc.

Roberts, P. (2008). *Mummy Portraits from Roman Egypt.* London: The British Museum Press.

Stavitsky, G. (1997). *Waxing Poetic: Encaustic Art in America.* Montclair, New Jersey: The Montclair Art Museum.

Taylor, W. B. (1843). *A Manual of Fresco and Encaustic Painting.* London: Chapman Hall.

About the Author

Kassandra Kelly never thought her first book would be a nonfiction DIY art materials book. She can most often be found tucked behind the covers of a ghost story or murder mystery, the spookier the better. She received her B.A. from Reed College and her M.F.A. from Pacific University. She lives in rural solitude with two dogs, a shameful number of cats (okay, five), ten thousand Italian honeybees, and one partner affectionately known as The Theory. Probably to hide his identity. Visit Kassandra at KassandraKelly.com or the Hive Encaustic blog at http://hive-encaustic.com/.

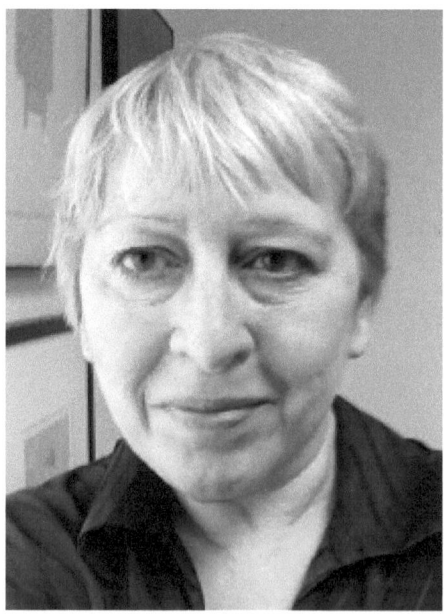